MANSA MUSA

AND THE
EMPIRE OF MALI

P. JAMES OLIVER

The design on the cover of this book features Mali's famous mud architecture. In the 1300s, Mansa Musa and his friend As-Sāhilī revolutionized architecture in Mali and across the rest of the Sudan by introducing the use of sun-dried mud bricks and a style that became known as the Malian style of architecture. The skyline on the cover is a collage of mud brick structures dating from the 1300s to the present.

ISBN-10: 146805354X
EAN-13: 9781468053548

TABLE OF CONTENTS

PREFACE

SOUTH OF THE SAHARA DESERT, long before the first Europeans arrived, three great empires existed in West Africa. One after another, these powerful merchant empires, rich in gold and skilled in commerce, prospered in relative isolation for hundreds of years.

Shown at their greatest extent

Empire of Ghana (700 – 1200 AD)

Separated from the rest of the world by the vastness of the Sahara Desert and a coastline sailors had not yet learned to navigate, only a sparse network of trade routes connected these great black African empires with their markets in the old world.

Empire of Mali (1200 – 1500AD)

Ghana, the first of the three empires, began in 700 A.D., as Europe lay deeply mired in the Dark Ages and Islam virtually exploded across North Africa, Europe and Asia. Much

Empire of Songhai (1350 – 1600 AD)

5

more slowly, Islam made its way to West Africa. Adopted primarily by prominent urban families, Islam stimulated Ghana's already vigorous gold trade. In 1312, as the Crusades ended and the Spice Trade which was to create such a huge demand for gold began, Kankan Musa became the Emperor of Mali, the second of the three empires.

From the pyramids to the Mona Lisa, from the *Iliad* to the Great Wall of China, the achievements of the world's greatest civilizations are wonderfully diverse. Stable, prosperous, powerful, long-lived, West Africa's merchant empires rank among the world's finest civilizations. Within each of them, exceptional individuals lifted their culture to greatness. Kankan Musa—Renaissance man, emperor and traveler—was such a person.

A JOURNEY

KANKAN MUSA AND HIS UNCLE STOOD QUIETLY on the beach watching as more than one hundred men loaded the many ships. Large mounds of food, gold and gear were piled on the beach to outfit the small vessels. Though the men were excited about the upcoming voyage, they worked slowly and with extraordinary care. Each of the two thousand ships needed enough supplies to sustain the crew in case they became separated from the others, yet it was imperative they not be overloaded. Every strip of dried meat, each coil of rope, could mean the difference between survival and despair.

The arrow shows the area they set sail from.

The year was 1312. Kankan's uncle, the Emperor of Mali, was about to embark on an exciting expedition. Though he was the ruler of a powerful empire, his passion was exploration. For years he had longed to know what, if anything, lay on the other side of the Western Ocean. A few years earlier, he had equipped 400 ships and instructed his captains not to return until they had run out of food or had reached the end of the ocean. A long time passed, and then one ship returned. In a state of great excitement, Kankan's uncle asked the captain what news he brought. "Your Majesty," the captain reported, "we traveled for a long time until there appeared in the open sea what seemed to be a river with a powerful current. My ship was last. The other ships went on ahead, but they did not return and we did not see them again. So, I turned about and did not enter that river." The emperor did not believe his captain's story and became vehement about trying again.[1]

Now, with his plans nearly complete, Kankan's uncle looked about with pleasure. He would be leading this expedition himself! He'd done some sailing before, but like most men of his day, he had always stayed within sight of the land. His dream was to sail straight out to sea, straight toward the place where the summer sun set. He didn't know if he would find land or if the ocean just went on forever. His journey could bring him fortune and fame, or he could be leading his ships to their doom, falling one after another off the edge of the world.

All he knew for sure was that such a voyage would be dangerous. Turning to Kankan, he said, "Nephew, son of my sister, in accordance with our people's customs, if I do not return from this voyage, you will become the next Emperor of Mali. If this should occur . . ."

Kankan's uncle never returned. Some historical records indicate that he, or at least some of the men who sailed with him, did, in fact, reach the Americas long before Christopher Columbus arrived in 1492.[2]

Chapter 2
EBONY, IVORY AND THE LAW

SOON AFTER HIS UNCLE SET SAIL, Kankan and his wives and children moved into Mali's royal palace. Built around an immense courtyard in Niani, Mali's capital, the palace was a large, sprawling complex that served as both the emperor's home and the headquarters of Mali's government. In addition to the luxurious rooms Kankan's family enjoyed, the palace boasted many meeting areas and offices, guest rooms and servants' quarters, a well-equipped stable, and a cooking area large enough to feed several thousand people.

The emperor's throne, beautifully crafted from hard black ebony, sat on a rectangular platform at one end of the courtyard. Here the empire's business was conducted, its history recited, and its ceremonies performed. This was the heart of Mali. Two huge, gleaming ivory tusks stood beside the throne, one on each side, like sentinels standing guard. Behind the throne, whenever the emperor was present, a row of handsomely-dressed pages stood expectantly in a straight line. A servant held a large silk umbrella above the emperor's head, shading him from the sun. Other servants fanned him when the day was hot. A herald stood in front of him, repeating his words in a loud voice so everyone present could hear. Off to one side, a row of horses waited quietly in case the emperor should wish to ride.

When the royal court was in session, crowds gathered in front of the platform to watch and listen. Seated upon the throne, the emperor gave orders, listened to reports from his governors and military advisers, settled disputes, and ruled on questions of law. Though Kankan Musa first served as a temporary leader in his uncle's absence, in time he was officially recognized as Mali's new emperor. From then on he was called Mansa Kankan Musa, Mansa Musa, or simply "the Mansa," which means "the emperor."

Chapter 3
BANISHING THE BANDITS

MANSA KANKAN MUSA HAD PLANS! Now that he was emperor, he planned to strengthen the army, conquer more lands, and increase the empire's power and wealth. He wanted to get rid of the bandits who roamed across Mali's countryside, frightening travelers and hindering trade. He also hoped to bring people to Allah (the Arabic word for God) and peace to the land.

Perhaps his greatest challenge, however, would be the isolation his new position would bring. As Mali's emperor, he could not have any close friends. All his former friends would have to be treated equally, and somewhat impersonally, so that none of them, or their families, would feel they had more power or influence with the emperor than anyone else. Just the appearance of favoritism could lead to fighting between the powerful families of Mali, and even to the assassination or overthrow of the emperor himself.

Like every emperor of Mali, Mansa Musa would have a *dyeli* who would serve as his counselor and friend, official mouthpiece or herald, and master of ceremonies at court functions and festivals. His *dyeli* would recite the *Epic of Old Mali* in public and compose the portion of the epic that would record the events of Mansa Musa's reign. As the "writer" of Mali's history, *dyelis* were feared and sometimes even despised because, though they could praise, they could also criticize. In addition to their other duties, *dyelis* were trained in constitutional procedures and were used to settle disputes arising between clans and tribes. Their role was both sensitive and important. To help assure their reliability, *dyelis* were chosen, in part, because of their low social status. This meant they would be dependent upon "their" emperor and would not have any kinsmen among the nobility or the freemen who might try to influence them or make a claim to the throne. Only with his *dyeli* would the Mansa be able to speak freely, get angry, or seek advice.

Well prepared, Mansa Musa handled the demands of his new position exceptionally well. People liked him. They felt he was fair. His superb administrative skills were apparent to all who worked under him, and his reputation as a great military leader grew with each campaign. His wisdom was reflected in every decree he made—and even in some he reversed.

For example, early in his reign, in an effort to convert people to Islam*, he ordered the gold miners in the South to stop practicing their pagan customs and to adopt the Muslim** way of life. The miners,

Stories tell of one especially memorable nugget that was so big an emperor used it to tether his horse.

---

*   Islam is the world religion founded by the Prophet Muhammad.

**   A Muslim is a believer in Islam

unwilling to give up their old customs, became so angry they protested his orders by drastically reducing their production of gold.

Every nugget of gold the mines produced went straight into the empire's treasury—the miners were only allowed to keep the gold dust and flakes. The angry miners were well aware that if they severely limited their production, the flow of gold into the empire's treasury would be dramatically reduced and sorely missed.

Instead of sending troops to force the miners to obey his wishes, Mansa Musa decided to allow the miners to return to their old ways. The miners, who understood their position as a subject people, as well as the value of their labor to the empire's financial health, went back to work. Thus a difficult and costly war was avoided, and Mali's people learned that the Mansa was wise enough and brave enough to publicly change his mind when it was in the empire's best interest.

Mansa Musa's most important victory was over the bandits who roamed the countryside.

The miners were skilled jungle fighters.

For years these bandits had crippled travel and trade. As emperor, he refused to tolerate roadside robbery and the bandits met with swift and certain punishment. Once the bandits were gone, trade flourished and Mali's marketplaces became filled with wonderful and exotic products from distant lands. Along with their merchandise, the traders brought news of the world, thrilling stories of adventure, and tales of strange and faraway places.

For the people of Mali, life was good. They lived in peace, food was plentiful, they felt free to travel, and their marketplaces were both exciting and prosperous.

Chapter 4
SANDALS AND HORSES AND THINGS: A REALITY-BASED IMAGINARY DAY

Market Day was a day to look forward to—an out-of-the-ordinary, who-knows-what-might-happen sort of day, a get-up-early, how-do-I-look, news-and-gossip, let's-get-going kind of day.

EAGER TO GET AN EARLY START on this important day, people entered Niani's marketplace just as the sun began to color the eastern sky. The traders, always among the first to arrive, visited with each other while they set out their goods. Local farmers and craftsmen, who also liked to come early, arrived from every direction and proudly, hopefully, displayed their goods. Soon, the first cheerful notes of the musicians could be heard. Then crowds of men, women and children filled the marketplace with noise and excitement. They came for supplies, a special something, or just to have a good time. It seemed like everyone in and around Niani was somehow involved.

One such person, a young sandal maker who lived in a small village just outside Niani, left his house a little before dawn with a load of sandals on his back and dreams of great trades in his head. All morning long he called out with gusto, "See how well these sandals are made. The leather is soft and smooth, yet very strong." By noon he had already traded seven pair for rice, millet, honey, dates, a few small tools and a handsome length of cotton woven by a friend of his. Later he traded three pair to a trader for gold, and another two pair, one to a potter and one to a dyer, for salt. Before the day ended, he exchanged the salt and gold (both of which were used as we use money) for enough leather to make another load of sandals.

As well as making good trades, the young sandal maker loved the excitement of an important market day. There were goods from as far away as China, India and Spain to see and touch and taste. Hundreds of people crowded into the marketplace: traders, farmers, craftsmen, hunters, entertainers, and ordinary people in search of supplies. The resulting swirl of colors, sounds, and drifting odors excited him. He liked to hear the traders' stories, watch the jugglers and dancers perform, and listen to the musicians play. In addition to all this, the chance to see his friends and catch up on what was going on in the city made the day wonderfully eventful.

In the 1300s, kola nuts were highly prized for their ability to relieve thirst. By the late 1900s, they were found around the world as an ingredient in Coca-Cola.[3]

As he walked home that evening, he felt proud that already he could hold his own during the tough bargaining that led to a good trade. He was also proud of the supplies his work had earned for himself and his family. In the distance, he watched a caravan of traders as they filed along a dusty trail. He imagined that they, too, had had a good day. If so, many of their packs were probably full of gold and ivory, beautifully tanned leather, lengths of cotton cloth and the kola nuts so many Arabs liked to chew. When the traders disappeared from view, he watched the birds and felt content.

While his people were busy trading in Niani's marketplace, the Mansa was busy overseeing a large trade with some Arabian-horse traders. Just the day before, the traders had arrived and set up camp a few miles outside Niani. The Mansa was anxious to see the herd, hoping it would be as fine as the men had promised.

Happy and excited, in the way a young child is before a big holiday, the Mansa woke up early. After a quick meal, he mounted one of his own Arabian horses, a beautiful bay, and rode out to where the caravan was camped. As he and several officers from Mali's cavalry approached the herd, he saw hundreds of sleek young horses milling about, grazing where the grass was long enough, or frolicking in small groups (first here, then there). Their coats created a giant quilt of soft grays mixed with rich chestnut, brown and almost golden tones, all of which were accented by patches of snow white and jet black.

The Mansa, who was an excellent rider, already owned several Arabians and knew their capabilities well. He also knew that the strength of Mali's cavalry, 10,000 riders strong, depended as much upon the speed and endurance of its horses as upon the skills of its riders.

By the end of the day, a bargain had been struck with the traders, and the Mansa had selected eleven superb young horses to add to the royal stable. The rest of the herd would belong to the cavalry. Almost all of the horses, the Mansa and the officers agreed, would become strong enough and fast enough to ride into battle.

Mali's cavalry—the military's elite corps—served under the direct orders of the Mansa himself. Charging across the grasslands in tight formation, they were largely unstoppable.

Cavalrymen wore headpieces of copper, chain-mail, or thick cloth turbans; a "shirt" of chain-mail or quilt-mail; and rode Arab, Barb, or an old breed of Saracen horses. These imported horses were very expensive. The horses the Sudanese bred were, for some reason, too small.

Though the Mansa may not have ridden out to view the horses himself, he did maintain direct communication with foreign traders throughout his empire, and had commercial agents empowered to buy from them before they could sell to anyone else. This gave the Mansa a nearly monopolistic control over imports and exports of strategic importance such as metals and horses.[4]

Chapter 5
AN OUNCE OF GOLD FOR AN OUNCE OF SALT

MINING, AGRICULTURE, AND TRADE formed the basis of Mali's economy. Its mines, both those within Mali proper and those under Mali's control, produced large quantities of high-quality gold, copper, and salt. Its farmers, ranchers, and fishermen all became increasingly productive and diversified under the Mansa's leadership. This provided Mali's people with a varied and plentiful stock of healthy foods and a large supply of cotton and leather. It was trade, however, that grew most dramatically during his reign.

Mansa Musa's focus on securing the countryside paid off. With the bandits gone and the constant threat of robbery and physical injury over, the traders celebrated by extending their routes across all of Mali's lands. They began to carry more and more goods and to earn ever-larger profits. As word of their riches spread, more traders came to Mali. They brought goods from as far away as Europe, India, Persia, and even China.

In return for silks and spices from China, sharp knives and small hand tools from Europe, exquisite Persian brocades, Arabian horses, and all the other marvelous goods the traders brought, they received valuable loads of gold, copper, cotton cloth, and other fine products from Mali. As the traders prospered, Mali prospered. Every load of goods the traders carried into or out of Mali was taxed by the empire, and so the empire grew rich. As the traders began to carry more goods and as the number of traders increased, the empire grew very rich.

One of the most lucrative trade routes in Mali linked the salt mines of Taghaza and the gold mines of Wangara. Salt was an important and highly valued commodity in Mali. It was used to season food, preserve meat, prevent dehydration and was essential in caring for livestock. However, every year heavy rains washed the salt out of Mali's soil and carried it to the sea. Since these rains prevented salt deposits from forming within its boundaries, Mali had to "import" salt from Taghaza.

Although the town of Taghaza was controlled by Mali, it was located far to the north of Mali proper in a flat, sandy portion of the Sahara Desert. Taghaza didn't have any trees or plants, just sand, the small homes of the miners, and the salt mines which lay beneath the sand.

Salt that was whiter than the whitest marble was taken from the mines in heavy, naturally occurring, regularly shaped blocks. While almost all of the salt was carried south by traders, some of the blocks were used to build the walls of the miners' homes. The roofs were made of stretched camel skins.

The traders would load their camels with salt and walk south for many weeks. Leading a long line of camels across the sand was hard, often scorchingly hot, dry, boring work. All day long the men had to keep walking. If they stopped to sit down for even a few minutes, their camels would also sit down and the salt would slide off their backs and onto the sand. At night, the weary men hobbled their camels and let them forage, but even when hobbled a camel would sometimes wander far away from camp. Each time this happened, it could cost the trader many hours of travel time just to find his camel and lead it back to camp.

When the traders finally reached the southern edge of the desert, they entered a "port" city. Just as in today's seaports, where goods are unloaded from ships and onto trucks, in these port cities goods were unloaded from camels and onto donkeys. In Mali, camels were best for transporting goods in the desert, donkeys were better in the grasslands, and human porters were essential in the equatorial forests. Although both camels and horses were used in central Mali, the traders who traveled south all the way to the edge of the equatorial forest always used donkeys because they were seldom affected by the bite of the tsetse fly.[*]

When bitten by a host[*] tsetse fly:

| camels usually died; | cattle usually died; | people frequently contracted sleeping sickness and died; | but donkeys were seldom affected. |

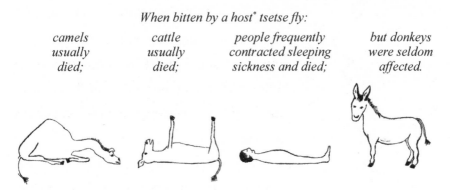

---

[*]   A host tsetse fly's blood contains trypanosomes, a parasite that causes disease. Most tsetse flies are host flies. See Tsetse fly in Glossary for more.

Taghaza

northern port city

Southern port city

secret trading sites

Mali's port cities buzzed with activity. Some traders scoured the marketplace buying food and gear for their next trip while others rested and visited with each other. They all had to meet with one of the empire's tax collectors while in the port city. Most importantly, this was where the traders met to trade with each other. Though most of them carried at least small quantities of other goods, salt and gold were the principal items exchanged along the Taghaza-Wangara trade route.

While the traders from Taghaza traded their salt for gold from Wangara, those from the south who had led long lines of donkeys loaded with gold clear across the vast grasslands of central Mali exchanged their gold for salt. The general rate of exchange was an ounce of gold for an ounce of salt, but quality, scarcity, demand and a trader's bargaining skills could affect the terms of a trade. With each man's profit and pride at stake, the bargaining between them often became intense.

When their business in the port city was complete, the traders from Taghaza loaded their camels with gold and returned to the desert. Those from the south loaded salt

The *Empire of Mali* *at its greatest extent*

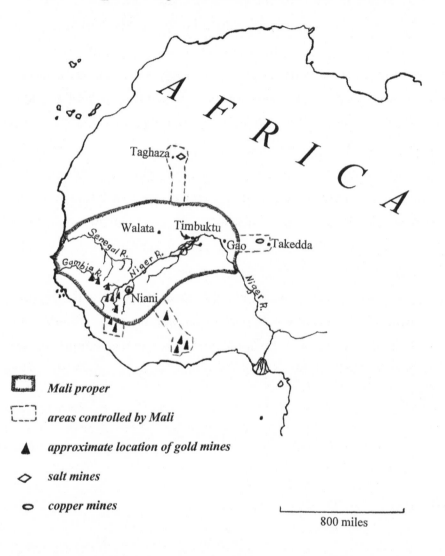

Mali proper

areas controlled by Mali

▲ **approximate location of gold mines**

◇ **salt mines**

○ **copper mines**

800 miles

onto their donkeys and headed back across the vast grasslands of central Mali. While traders were free to vary their travels, most chose to retrace the same route over and over again. Their families often lived at one end of the route. Also, those with camels were generally desert people while those with donkeys lived in the grasslands.

When the traders with the salt reached the southern edge of Mali's grasslands, they came to one of the southern port cities. To the south was the dark, dense, difficult, equatorial forest. The port cities of the south served much the same function as their northern counterparts. Here, too, one means of transporting goods was exchanged for another, taxes were paid, supplies replenished, and salt was traded for gold.

The next group of traders to buy the salt had long lines of human porters. Balancing heavy loads on their heads, these porters carried salt and other supplies to the gold miners of Wangara. Walking single file along the narrow trails that crisscrossed the dense forest, the porters traveled hundreds of miles to secret sites near the gold mines. At one of these secret places hidden deep in the forest, the traders exchanged their goods for the miners' gold.

Thus, salt traveled south and gold moved north along the Taghaza-Wangara trail. This was just one of many such routes. Mali's entire system of trade routes, taxation, and international commerce was as complex and highly organized as any system known before the mid-1900s.[5]

Chapter 6

9,000 MILES

TWELVE YEARS AFTER BECOMING MALI'S EMPEROR, the Mansa, like his uncle before him, decided to leave Mali and embark on a long journey. The empire was at peace. Trade was flourishing, people's lives were good, the empire was considerably larger and stronger, and Mali's government was becoming very wealthy indeed. In fact, Mali had entered its Golden Age. Unlike his uncle, however, the Mansa didn't dream of sailing out to sea on a voyage of discovery, but instead wanted to ride across the world's largest desert, around the Red Sea, and down the coast of the Arabian Peninsula to Mecca.

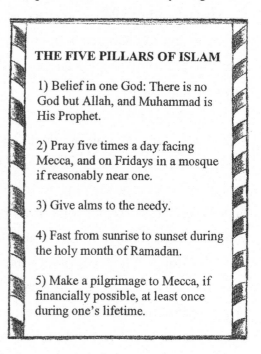

THE FIVE PILLARS OF ISLAM

1) Belief in one God: There is no God but Allah, and Muhammad is His Prophet.

2) Pray five times a day facing Mecca, and on Fridays in a mosque if reasonably near one.

3) Give alms to the needy.

4) Fast from sunrise to sunset during the holy month of Ramadan.

5) Make a pilgrimage to Mecca, if financially possible, at least once during one's lifetime.

A devout Muslim, Mansa Musa wanted to go to Mecca so he could participate in the religious observances held there. The trip would be long and difficult, over 9,000 miles, but if at all possible every Muslim should make at least one pilgrimage to Mecca.

"I want you to make all the preparations that will be needed for my pilgrimage," the Mansa told an assistant. "I am eager to begin my journey. So, starting tomorrow, you and your staff are to devote your-selves solely to making the necessary arrangements."

Many months later, on a day believed to be good for beginning a long journey, the Mansa's royal pilgrimage to Mecca began. On this momentous occasion, the Mansa wore an especially wide pair of pants. The wider a person's pair of pants, the greater their status in Mali's society, so Mansa Musa's pants were the widest worn in all of Mali. Wide in the seat and narrow in the leg, they were made from a rich fabric only the emperor was allowed to wear. Splendidly dressed, the Mansa left his palace and mounted a powerful black stallion that had been lavishly adorned with gold trappings. When he rode out to greet the huge crowd that had gathered outside the palace walls, he looked magnificent!

The crowd was in a festive mood. A feeling of celebration, of shared adventure, and of awe engulfed them as they stood watching the tremendous caravan begin to assemble. They had come to see the Mansa off and to say goodbye to friends who would be leaving with him. When the Mansa emerged from behind the palace wall, a loud wave of excited, cheering voices burst from the crowd.

After stopping to acknowledge the crowd, the Mansa, filled with excitement and a deep sense of pleasure, swung his horse around and headed north. Sixty thousand people left with him. Sixty thousand! Most of them would walk all the way to Mecca and then all the way back. Others, like the Mansa, had horses to ride. Some were guests, but a great many were servants. Eight thousand were soldiers who had been selected from Mali's army of 100,000. Several of the guests were governors or other leaders who might try to take over the government while the Mansa was away, and so they had been invited to come along. Some were members of the royal family. Others were simply Muslims from Mali who wanted to make their own pilgrimage and needed the protection the Mansa's large caravan provided. An essential few were guides.

Many of the travelers were lavishly dressed in bold cottons or imported fabrics set off by gold or silver jewelry. Many had delicate strands of gold woven into their hair, their clothing, and even into their horses' manes. The Mansa's personal servants, 12,000 in all, wore colorful brocades or silks from Persia. Five hundred of them, each of whom carried an ornamental staff made of gold, walked as a unit just in front of where he rode.

Hundreds of horses and long, long lines of camels formed the backbone of the caravan. Excited by all the activity, the horses were eager to get started. The camels were not. (Camels do not like to work. While being loaded, they often spit at, bite, or even kick the person tying on their packs. When the packs are secure, they grunt and groan loudly while getting to their feet, but once they are up and moving they will usually walk patiently for many hours.) All the food, water, tents, tools, clothing, cooking utensils, and gold the caravan would need was loaded on the camels' backs.

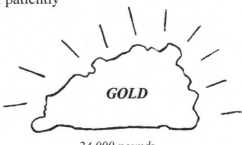

24,000 pounds

Eighty of the camels carried nothing but gold—three hundred pounds each! All of this gold, some of which had been made into fine jewelry or beautiful goblets, constituted the Mansa's "traveling" bank account. He would use it to buy additional supplies and to give away as gifts to a great many of the people he'd meet while on his pilgrimage.

By late afternoon, Niani was behind them. The broad grasslands of central Mali lay ahead. Once the caravan was moving, it became a long, slender line of life, color, and glittering gold that stretched for miles across the landscape. All along its route, people stopped what they were doing to stare.

Chapter 7
A DELIGHT

FOR THE MANSA, TRAVELING ACROSS the grasslands of central
Mali was a delight. Herds of elephants, giraffes, and gazelles roamed
the vast open spaces. Fields of grain, cotton, peanuts, and other crops
grew wherever there was enough water. The wide, wan-
dering Niger River shimmered in the bright sunlight, and
almost daily he saw sunrises and sunsets that were rich
with color. Best of all, he could gallop off on short
side trips and then easily and safely rejoin the
caravan which couldn't travel faster than three
to four miles per hour—the speed at which
people walk.

Once, while riding qui-
etly with a few friends, he
saw a huge bull elephant
with its ears spread
wide. From the tip
of one ear to the
tip of the other was

the learners   *the lookout*

31

ten feet. The huge ears of such an elephant, if killed for meat, were saved and used to make the skins for Mali's royal drums.

Another time, the Mansa laughed aloud as he sat watching some young giraffes struggle to learn the trick to getting a drink of water. With such a long neck, it seems like it would be easy for a giraffe to just reach down and get a drink, but a giraffe's legs are even longer than its neck! So, each young giraffe must learn how to stand in that funny, spraddle-legged position all giraffes use when getting a drink. Early one morning, the Mansa stopped to watch some lion cubs at play. Later that day, he rode hard beside a swiftly running herd of antelope. These side trips were fun. On them, he saw much of Mali's countryside and met many of its people.

One day, with a small group of men, he rode east for several hours to meet with a local official. When they entered the man's house, they saw that his children were chained up. "I'm having them memorize the Koran (the holy book of Islam), but lately they've been progressing much too slowly! I'll let them loose as soon as they've got it memorized," the official remarked as he seated his guests.

This man's method of "encouragement" was occasionally used by Muslim parents. Since books were scarce and very valuable, some parents believed it was essential that their children learn the Koran by heart so that its guidance and comfort would always be with them. The Koran is only a little shorter than the Christian New Testament, yet thousands of Muslim children memorized the whole book.

Another time, after a long hard ride, the Mansa and some friends stopped to cool off under a wild baobab tree. This ancient tree was so big that dozens of mounted riders could cool off in its shade. In addition to enjoying the shade of baobab trees, Mali's people made bread, red dye, and a medicine that helped them survive in the tropics from these grand old trees. On this day, however, the Mansa was not interested in any of these things. What he was really hoping to find was some clear, cool water.

Baobab trees can live to be a thousand years old. The trunks of very old trees can reach 30 feet in diameter. As the years pass, the central portion of these huge tree-trunks often rot away. Each year, when the rains come, the rotten portion of the trunk fills with water and rots a little more. Year after year the rotting continues until some of these old trees can hold many gallons of water.

In this particular tree, instead of water the Mansa found a young man hard at work. One side of the tree's trunk had been damaged, and the gnarly-edged opening in its side had widened enough to let the water flow out and the young man come in. The clever fellow had set up a loom in the tree's cool, small-bedroom-sized hollow and was busily weaving his cotton into cloth. Just as the weaver enjoyed his shady workplace, the Mansa enjoyed telling the story of the young man he'd found in a tree.

Chapter 8
A PERILOUS EXPANSE

WHEN THE CARAVAN REACHED THE SOUTHERN EDGE of the Sahara Desert, traveling became more difficult and more dangerous. The Mansa's casual side trips ended. Enormous stretches of sand and dunes lay ahead. Further on they would have to cross mile after mile after mile of barren, rocky ground. Every day the glare and heat from the sun baked the land. In the summer, the temperature could soar above 130 degrees Fahrenheit, and the rock-covered ground could reach 170 degrees. At night, the air temperature dropped rapidly—often falling close to 100

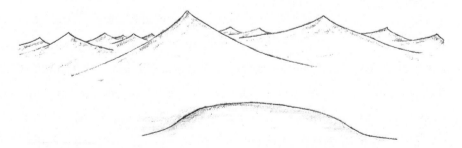

In 1964, Theodore Monod and his Bedouin guide came upon an "irregular elevation" in the sand. Digging down, they uncovered the remains of a camel caravan loaded with 2' long copper rods that had been buried by a sandstorm in the 11ᵗʰ or 12ᵗʰ century.

degrees below its daytime high. Only during one of the Sahara's rare rainstorms or, much more frequently, during a sandstorm that filled the air with wind-driven sand that slashed at everything and everyone, was the sun hidden.

This vast, dry, hot, barren land is punctuated by widely scattered oases where water bubbles to the surface and creates an island of green. Except at these oases, and a smattering of water holes, there isn't any water; without water, death comes quickly in the Sahara. Therefore, whenever possible, the caravan stopped to replenish its supply of water and to let each of its members, both the animals and the people, drink their fill. A thirsty camel can drink about 25 gallons of water in just ten minutes, and after a good drink it can live for days or weeks—even for months depending upon the weather—without another drink. A thirsty person, on the other hand, can only drink a few cups of water at

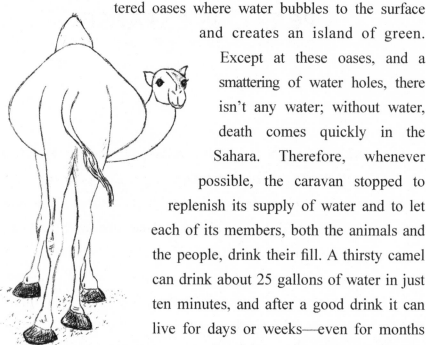

*The dimensions of this camel were taken from a photo of a camel that had just finished drinking his fill. He's **not** pregnant.*

a time, and will need another drink within a few hours. Every adult in the caravan needed at least a gallon of water a day. Because it could take days and sometimes even weeks for the caravan to travel from one oasis to the next, the Mansa's servants loaded hundreds of thousands of gallons of water onto the camels at each oasis.

Between oases, there were no roads or visible trails. Day after day, the travelers were surrounded by rocky landscapes that looked about the same in one place as in another or by vast stretches of sand dunes that changed each time the wind blew. Most of the time, there were no landmarks to guide a person who became separated from the caravan, so such a separation usually meant death. Yet, the highly skilled guides who led the caravan were able to keep it on course by studying the positions of the stars (much as sailors used to do), the sun's path across the sky, and the patterns the wind left in the sand.

When the caravan reached the central portion of the Sahara, it passed close to the hottest place on Earth. In this tremendously hot region, there is a vast, rugged, arid plateau, the Tassili n' Ajjer Plateau, that is covered with severely eroded, often eerie-looking rock formations, caves, and steep-sided gullies. Tassili n' Ajjer is a silent, largely lifeless place, yet hundreds of beautiful rock paintings have been discovered there. They were painted 2,000 to 8,000 years ago by artists who lived in the Sahara when it was lush and green. Then, ever so gradually, this vast land of rushing rivers and fertile valleys dried up and became the hot, desolate desert the Mansa and his caravan were crossing.

How would you feel *if you were out exploring one of the hottest, driest, most desolate places on earth and you suddenly came upon thousands of paintings of elephants and giraffes and rabbits and cows and people on the rocks and in the caves all around you? This is what happened to Dr. Henri Lhote, a French explorer-ethnologist, in 1956.*[6]

Following his discovery of the Tassili n' Ajjer rock paintings, Henri Lhote and a team of artists spent 16 months reproducing 800 of the paintings. After sponging off a scene with water carried in by camel, the scene was traced and then painted. Great care was taken to match the rich colors used by the ancient artists.

part of a court scene

a shepherd

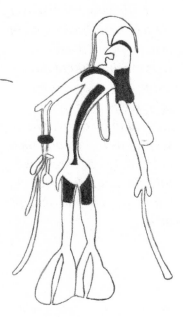

a dancer

hairdos from Tassili n' Ajjer

The diverse populations portrayed in the paintings migrated to other lands as their homeland dried up.

an injured or exhausted warrior falls

The rock paintings are remarkably beautiful. Their lines are simple and elegant, the colors rich and earthy. (All I can show you here are a few small drawings.) Among the actual rock paintings are images of rhinoceroses 25' long and elephants 15' tall.

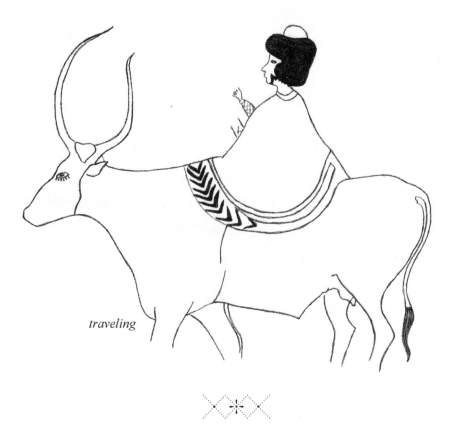

traveling

In spite of the desert's heat, its barren terrain, and its apparent end-lessness, at the end of each day's travel, every member of the caravan received an elaborately prepared meal, compliments of the Mansa and his large corps of excellent cooks. These incredible meals were served at each stopping place along the entire route from Mali to Mecca. After the meal and perhaps some entertainment, the travelers slept.

The next day, fed and rested, the caravan filed out across the desert until it became, once again, a long slender "creature" that crept across the desert at human walking speed. Many hours later, tired and hungry, it would scrunch up, have another elaborate meal, and sleep. In this way, day after day after day, the caravan slowly crept across the mighty Sahara, a perilous expanse of dry, barren land that is almost as large as the entire United States of America.

Sahara Desert: about 3,500,000 sq. miles
United States: 3,618,276 sq. miles
(all 50 states).

Chapter 9
A LASTING IMPRESSION

"THERE'S CAIRO!" AMID SHOUTS OF EXCITEMENT, the travelers jumped to their feet and peered out across the desert. In the evening, the city hadn't been visible, but now, with the pre-dawn sun lighting the sky behind it, they could just make out the city's skyline. Its solid black silhouette was framed by a delicate pink and yellow glow. It was a beautiful sight. A few minutes later, the brilliance of the rising sun hid the city from view.

That glimpse of Cairo filled the Mansa with excitement. Finally, the first long leg of his journey was almost over. Soon he would be inside the great city of Cairo, a city few of Mali's people had seen, but that almost all of them had heard about from the traders. By the time he actually entered the city, his excitement had become intense.

Magnificently dressed and surrounded by the splendor of his caravan, Mansa Kankan Musa, Emperor of Mali, entered the city's majestic western gate and rode into Cairo. Almost automatically, a lane opened down the middle of the crowded street. People stopped whatever they were doing and stared in amazement at the incredibly spectacular leader of some unknown land who was riding slowly down their street. Directly in front of him marched a company of 500 colorfully dressed men, each of whom carried an ornamental staff made of gold. Stretched out behind him was an enormous, well-guarded caravan that dazzled every eye with its incredible display of gold and silver, gleaming jewels, and richly colored fabrics.

The excited voices of the people out in the street attracted the attention of those in the shops and buildings along the way. Hurrying outside, they, too, shouted and stared in amazement. Even the Egyptian official responsible for meeting incoming

The Mosque of an-Nasir Muhammad, under construction during the Mansa's visit to Cairo, is still standing within the walls of the Citadel.

caravans exclaimed, "In all my life, I've never seen anything like this. Why, this caravan competes in glittering glory with the African sun itself!"[7]

After the long months the Mansa had spent crossing the vast open spaces of the Sahara, the sudden whirl of big city sights, sounds, crowds, colors, commotion and attention was exhilarating. He had planned to rest, to bathe in clear, scented water, and to sip cool drinks as soon as he reached Cairo, but with all the excitement surrounding his arrival, his desire to rest vanished. All he wanted now was to revel in the sights and sounds and wonders of this great city.

Cairo was a large, vibrant city. Nearly a million people lived there, and many more came to study under its teachers, trade in its famous markets, and visit its superb libraries, mosques, hospitals, and observatories. Tourists came to see the pyramids, its ancient works of art, the Nile River, and the gleaming marble Citadel whose thick walls protected the Sultan's palace.

Soon after the Mansa's arrival, the Sultan of Egypt held a grand celebration to welcome him. However, when

Building Cairo's Citadel

All those doing the hard labor—sizing the marble, cutting the huge shaft through solid rock, and cutting away (by hand with pickaxes) tons of rock from the base of the Citadel's exterior walls—were Christian Europeans. Captured during the Crusades, these prisoners of war, used as forced laborers, were so numerous their "numbers were beyond computation."[8]

45

the Mansa arrived at the sultan's palace and was told that all guests of the sultan were expected to kiss the sultan's hand or the ground before his throne, he refused. "How can it be that I am being asked to pay homage to a man?" he asked. "Am I not on my pilgrimage? I've come to praise Allah, and only Allah!" Also, although he was too polite to say so, he knew that his empire was larger than the sultan's, and that his wealth in terms of gold was far greater.

Finally, a wise member of the Mansa's court suggested that the Mansa kiss the ground in praise of Allah, the creator of all things. After the Mansa did so, the Sultan of Egypt stood up and invited the Emperor of Mali to come forward and sit beside him. Once they were seated, the two men had a long and friendly conversation. Although the Mansa usually chose to use an interpreter, he spoke Arabic fluently. At the end of the celebration, the sultan gave the Mansa many fine gifts and graciously provided a place for him, and his entire caravan, to stay while they were in Cairo.

For three months they rested and waited for the worst heat of summer to pass. During these months, the people of Cairo learned who Mansa Musa was and where he'd come from. They saw the dignity with which he conducted himself and observed the exemplary behavior of his followers. They heard about his trustworthiness, his devotion to his pilgrimage, and the size and power of his empire. They saw the respect with which his followers, and their own sultan, treated him. Most exciting and talked about, though, were his striking style of dress and his incredible generosity.

Everywhere he went during his stay in Cairo, the Mansa gave away gold. He gave it away as gifts, distributed it as alms, and spent it generously in the marketplace. In fact, he gave away so much gold that the price of gold in and around the city dropped dramatically and stayed well below normal for more than twelve years!

Stories about his amazing generosity flew around Cairo. Almost as popular were the stories about Mali's stupendous supply of gold, the splendor and immensity of its royal caravan, and the incredibly magnificent emperor who wore those wonderfully wide, vibrantly colored pants.

People loved these stories. They marveled in amazement when they heard them and reveled in their glory when they told them. For centuries, these stories were told and retold until they became almost like legends.

Chapter 10
"WE MADE IT – PRAISE BE TO ALLAH"

RESTED AND EAGER TO CONTINUE HIS JOURNEY, the Mansa left Cairo. There were still close to 1,000 miles of dry, rugged land to cross before he would reach Mecca, and since the religious observances he was traveling so far to participate in were only held once a year, he had to get there on time.

Soon after leaving Cairo, the Mansa and his caravan were in the desert again—the long, narrow, flat, gravelly desert that lies between the Nile River and the Red Sea. A few days later they reached the northern tip of the Gulf of Suez. Here, where the sand and rock of the desert meet the sandy shore of the gulf, they stepped out of Africa and into Asia.

Before them lay the Sinai Peninsula, a devastatingly barren triangle of land wedged between Africa and the enormous bulk of Asia. Far to the south, tall, rocky mountains reached into the sky, and far to the north, the beautiful Mediterranean Sea lapped against the coast. From where he rode, however, all the Mansa could see was sand, gravel, and a huge, arid, rocky plateau. This is such a frighteningly dry place that when Moses led his people into the Sinai, they threatened to revolt and return to the misery of slavery rather than face such desolation and what looked like certain starvation.

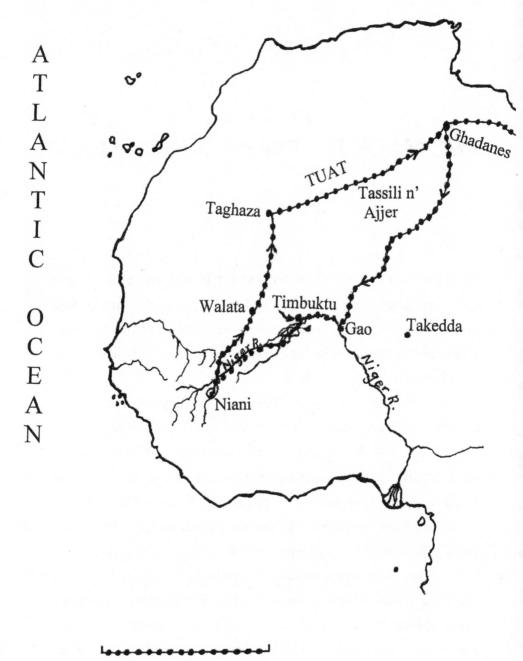

A T L A N T I C   O C E A N

Taghaza

TUAT

Tassili n' Ajjer

Ghadanes

Walata

Timbuktu

Gao

Takedda

Niger R.

Niger R.

Niani

Mansa Musa's route

MANSA MUSA'S ROUTE

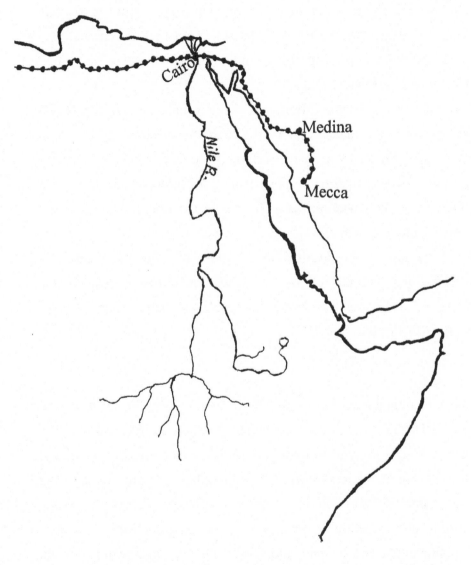

Niani→ Walata→ Taghaza→ Ghadames→ Cairo→ Mecca

Mecca→ Cairo→ Ghadames→ Gao→ Timbuktu→ Niani

At the northern end of the Gulf of Aqaba, the route to Mecca from Africa merged with the route from Europe and Asia. This was also where the Mansa and his caravan turned south and faced Mecca. Like all Muslims, the Mansa turned to face Mecca every time he knelt to pray. From here on, he would face Mecca all day long as he traveled, and this fact pleased him. So did the fact that they were getting close—only 800 more miles!

After the African and European-Asian routes merged, the Mansa saw people from places very unlike Mali. Never before had he seen or imagined such a variety of clothing, headgear, skin colors, or languages. All these people, from so many different lands, were also pilgrims on their way to Mecca. It was fascinating and exciting and rather humbling, somehow.

Like most of the pilgrims he saw along the way, the Mansa visited Medina. The city of Medina, whose name means "City of the Prophet," was named in honor of the Prophet Muhammad, the founder of the Muslim religion.

Muhammad was born into a well-respected family in or around 570 A.D., but he was soon orphaned. Though he lived most of his life in Mecca, he fled to Medina when he was about fifty years old because the merchants of Mecca had turned against him for speaking out against idol worship. For many years, these merchants had made a lot of money selling goods to the crowds that flocked to Mecca to worship in front of the many idols housed there, and they did not want their very profitable businesses ruined. So, when Muhammad refused to stop speaking out against idol worship, the merchants became so angry they threatened to kill him.

While still living in Mecca, Muhammad had a vision in which the angel Gabriel instructed him to go forth and "recite" in the name of Allah. Though terrified at first, Muhammad later became convinced that he had in fact been called by God to be His messenger. Upon many occasions over the next decade or more, Muhammad recited (spoke aloud) the words he "found in his heart," believing them to be from God. These revelations, and not Muhammad's everyday utterances, were remembered and recorded in the Koran, which Muslims believe to be the Word of God.

After fleeing to Medina, Muhammad continued teaching and preaching that Allah is the one and only God. At times, without willing it, he would fall into a trance and a torrent of rhythmic prose would flow from his lips. The people of Medina listened to him, and many of them came to believe that he truly was a prophet of Allah.

In addition to accepting him as a prophet, the people of Medina made him their governor. While serving as the city's governor, Muhammad worked hard to promote social justice and to establish peace within Medina. His conflict with Mecca, however, developed into a series of armed conflicts between his followers in Medina and the people of Mecca, which led to an intercity war.

After three years of intermittent, bloody battles, Mecca was defeated. Thus, only eight years after fleeing Mecca, Muhammad returned with a great many followers and destroyed all the pagan idols housed there. Contrary to the mores of his culture, Muhammad did not carry out a bloody revenge against the people of Mecca. Instead, following his victory, he established Mecca—the site of the Kaaba*,

---

* The Kaaba is a small, rectangular building that houses the sacred Black Stone, which, according to Muslim tradition, the angel Gabriel gave to Abraham. Muslims believe the Black Stone is a sign of Allah's covenant with Abraham.

the Mount of Mercy, and other sites important to Muslims—as the religious capital of Islam. Medina remained its political capital.

Only two and one-half years after his triumphant return to Mecca, Muhammad died. His body was enshrined in the Prophet's Mosque in Medina.

Like most Muslim pilgrims who visit Medina, the Mansa went to the Prophet's Mosque to pray in front of Muhammad's tomb. He also visited other mosques and shrines, enjoyed long conversations with some of the Muslim scholars he met there, and gave away a lot more gold.

When he left Medina for Mecca, the Mansa followed much the same route Muhammad had taken. After traveling south about 240 miles, the Mansa stopped atop the dry, rugged hills that surround Mecca. Looking back, he could see only segments of his caravan— a glittering band of bright colors stretched across a hillside here, another segment climbing up through a draw there. Little plant life grew on these stark hills, so even the more distant portions of his caravan were easy to see.

Suddenly he heard people shouting. "There it is!" "There's Mecca!" Turning around quickly, he rode forward, slid off his horse, and ran to join the excited people looking down at Mecca. Mecca! He'd dreamt of Mecca for so long. Now, standing there, lightheaded with joy and amazement, he felt exhilarated, and also deeply grateful.

"We made it! Praise be to Allah!" he exclaimed. Far below him, like the bull's-eye of a giant target, he could see the Kaaba. Around the Kaaba, the spacious courtyard of the Great Mosque lay smooth and inviting. Surrounding the courtyard was a tall white wall whose stately arches welcomed pilgrims from every direction. Beyond the wall stood the city of Mecca. Around the city, thousands of pilgrims had already pitched their tents. Beyond the thick ring of tents, a barren plain stretched to the foot of the brown hills that encircled the city. Teary-eyed, the Mansa looked down in wonder.

Before entering Mecca, pilgrims cleanse themselves and dress in seamless garments. In recognition of the facts that all people are equal before God and that many nomadic peoples did not have tailors, all men wore a simple garment consisting of two lengths of white cloth. Women traditionally wore long robes.

Chapter 11
THE HAJJ

*"Know ye that every Muslim is a brother unto every other Muslim,
and that ye are now one brotherhood."*

From Muhammad's Farewell Sermon

FOR THE TWELVE DAYS OF HIS PILGRIMAGE, the Mansa wore a plain, seamless, white garment identical to that worn by every other man.* Like them, he could not wear jewelry or other decorations, become involved in an argument or dispute, have sexual relations, or harm any living thing. With them, he would participate in the prayers, rituals, and celebrations of his pilgrimage, so that during these twelve wonderful days, he would be a brother to, instead of a ruler over, other men and women.

When he walked into the Great Mosque to participate in the first ritual of his pilgrimage, he was immediately absorbed by the crowd. He moved with it and became part of it. He forgot everything except the Kaaba, the sacred Black Stone, and the prayers being said. During

---

* Ināri Kunāte, the Mansa's first wife, wore a loose, white outer-garment and a headscarf much like those worn by the other women. Scholars don't mention whether the Mansa's other wives accompanied him on his pilgrimage. In fact, little is written about the women of Mali except to say that they were particularly beautiful, held a respected position in their society, and enjoyed many freedoms.

the days that followed, he participated fully and joyfully in all the events of his pilgrimage.

Following the climactic ninth day's "Greater Pilgrimage" on the Mount of Mercy, during which each pilgrim "stands before Allah" from noon until dusk, the Mansa spent the night in the open with all the other pilgrims. For the next three days they feasted. After the feasting, he returned to the courtyard of the Great Mosque and walked slowly around the Kaaba, then bent to kiss the sacred Black Stone one more time.

The Mansa was a hajji now. Hajji is the title given people who have completed their pilgrimage to Mecca. For the devout Muslim, there is no greater joy on earth.

After completing his pilgrimage, the Mansa stayed in Mecca to pray and to talk with many of the scholars he'd met there. Because only Muslims were allowed to enter Mecca, all the scholars were Muslims. Similarly, because only men could gather in public places, they were all men. In all other ways, however, they were a diverse group with wide-ranging interests and a rich variety of backgrounds, professions and homelands. Because the Mansa was also an educated man with many interests and talents, they welcomed him and listened to him with respect.

During these long and stimulating conversations, the Mansa learned a lot that was new to him about his religion, especially, but also about architecture, astronomy, law and agriculture. He heard about places, peoples, and forms of government that he had known little or nothing about. He went sightseeing, gave away a lot more gold, and spent time in prayer and meditation. His days were leisurely but full.

Happy and at peace, he wanted to stay in Mecca and make it his home, but he knew that his son, who was serving as Mali's emperor during his absence, was inexperienced and, according to the reports he'd been receiving, a weak and ineffective leader. Therefore, the Mansa felt he should return to Mali at least long enough to see for himself how well his son could govern. While he was trying to decide whether to return to Mali or stay in Mecca, a hard-riding messenger galloped into camp. Though exhausted, the messenger was immediately brought before the Mansa. Casting himself face-down upon the ground, as was the custom when addressing the emperor, he gasped, "Your Majesty, your army is engaged in combat with the Kingdom of Songhai!"

After announcing his news, the messenger was taken away and given water and food. A few hours later, the Mansa questioned him thoroughly in order to learn all he could about his army, the conflict, and the strategies of his commanding officers.

Early the next morning, the Mansa sent for his Chief Steward. "Prepare the caravan for travel," he ordered. "We are leaving Mecca." He had decided to return to Mali, assess the state of affairs there and in Songhai, and to initiate the projects he'd started thinking about during his long talks with the scholars. Then, if all went well in Mali, he could return to Mecca.

While the caravan was being prepared, he went into Mecca and invited some of the scholars to return to Mali with him. Several of them accepted his invitation. The most influential among them was a Moorish poet and architect from Granada, Abu Ishāq as-Sāhilī. As-Sāhilī, who was often referred to simply as "the Moor," and the Mansa had become good friends. So, when the Mansa found the Moor that day, he asked him with obvious eagerness, "Will you return to Mali with me? I need a man with your talents to help me make my dreams for Mali come true."

The Moor smiled and replied, "Your Majesty, I shall be honored to return with you and to help in any way I am able."

In addition to the scholars, the Mansa asked that some *shurafā*—descendants of the Prophet—accompany him back to Mali so that his people would be blessed whenever they saw them and the land blessed by their footprints. After a considerable amount of negotiation with the Grand *Sharif* of Mecca, four *shurafā* and their families decided to join the caravan and move to Mali.

Quickly and efficiently the Mansa's staff prepared the caravan for travel. So, within just a few days of his decision to return to Mali, the Mansa, his caravan, the scholars, and the *shurafā* left Mecca. They would go to Cairo first, purchase great quantities of supplies there, and then begin the long, grueling journey back across the Sahara.

The first few weeks of travel passed quickly for the Mansa because he and the Moor spent so many happy hours lost in conversation; but, as time passed, the Mansa grew impatient with the caravan's slow pace. Every day's journey was long and difficult, yet, at the end of each day, it didn't seem like they'd made much progress. After weeks of tedious travel, even Cairo, which was only one-fourth of the way to Niani, was still hundreds of miles away.

Chapter 12
A VAST "GOLDEN LAND"

MANSA MUSA AND MALI WERE FAMOUS—WORLD FAMOUS!
By the time the Mansa and his caravan reached Cairo, the stories about Mali, the Mansa, and his spectacular caravan that had kept tongues wagging so happily in Cairo had "flown" out of Cairo, sped across Northern Africa, around the Middle East and through the trading nations of Europe. Almost immediately, because of its reputed wealth and size, Mali was recognized as a world power, and the Mansa as one of the world's most splendid and powerful rulers.

Word of Mali's stupendous supply of gold, however, created the most excitement. Within just a few months, hundreds of governments, merchants and adventurers had become desperately anxious to reach this amazing "golden land," but they didn't know how to get there. No one seemed to know! The stories said Mali was "across the great desert" or "somewhere beyond the Sahara," but the Sahara was huge and dangerous and almost no one who heard the stories knew what lay beyond it.

There were, of course, some West African traders who knew how to reach Mali's gold country, but these traders kept their routes a secret, and even they never saw the gold mines or the miners they traded with. When making a trade, they carried their goods to secret meeting places deep in the forest and laid them on the ground. After beating on drums to signal the beginning of trade, they retreated half-a-day's journey from the trading site. When the trad- e r s had left the area, the gold miners came to the site. They looked over the goods, set what they hoped the traders would accept as a fair payment, all in gold, beside each trader's pile of goods, and then retreated half-a-day's journey into the forest. When the traders returned, they beat their drums to signal the end of trading if they were satisfied with the gold miner's payment. If not, they retreated again indicating that the min- ers must leave more gold. This process continued until both sides were satisfied. In this way, the miners received the supplies they needed and kept the location of their mines a secret.

Far away in Europe, the world's best mapmakers, spurred on by the demands of their clients for a map that included Mali, bus- ily set about gathering information. However, the information they needed was so difficult to obtain that 15 years passed before Angelino Dulcert correctly indicated Mali's location on a navigational chart, and another 36 years before Abraham Cresques completed an atlas for Charles V of France that included a map of Mali! Cresques' success was probably due to information he obtained from Jewish friends. Unlike Christians, whom the Muslims of North Africa refused to let cross their land because they were still bitter about the Crusades,

Jewish merchants were often allowed to cross. Like Columbus' voyages would a century later, Cresques' map dramatically expanded the boundaries of the known world.[9] It also added an additional level of credibility to the stories of gold and riches surrounding Mali.

In the 1300s, mapmakers customarily drew small pictures of important people on their maps. So, within the boundaries of Mali, Cresques drew a picture of Mansa Musa holding a golden scepter in one hand and a large gold nugget in the other.

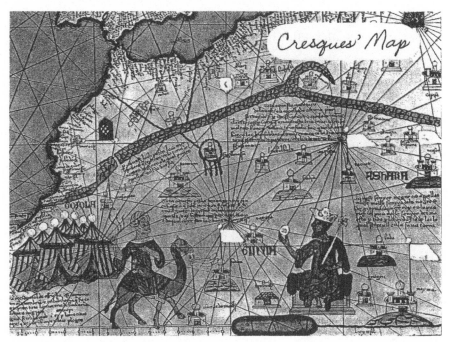

Mansa Musa's pilgrimage revealed the immensity of Mali's gold supply to the world.

Unaware of his new fame, the Mansa and his caravan re-entered Cairo. Just as crowds of people had gathered to stare at him when he first arrived, they rushed into the streets to see him now that he was back. His first visit had been a thrilling event, and the people of Cairo welcomed him with enthusiasm.

The Mansa was also glad to be back. It meant that one leg of his long journey back to Niani was finished. Although Cairo was their most important and interesting stopping place, the Mansa was eager to leave for Mali as soon as possible. Therefore, soon after they arrived, he sent for his Chief Steward. "Buy all the supplies the caravan will need for our journey as quickly as you can," he ordered. "I don't want to stay in Cairo any longer than necessary."

A few days later, after frantically scouring Cairo for good deals on the enormous quantities of food and other supplies the caravan would need, his distressed Chief Steward returned to the Mansa. "Your Majesty, there isn't enough gold left to purchase all the supplies we'll need!"

Surprised, and somewhat embarrassed, the Mansa knew he would have to find a way to borrow a large amount of gold. Word of his plight quickly reached the ears of Egypt's wealthy merchants. Almost immediately, they flocked to him and eagerly offered to loan him all the gold he needed—at a great rate of interest, of course. Though he was irritated as well as amused by their eagerness, he borrowed a large sum of gold from one of them, a sum he later paid back in full, at the princely rate of 700 dinar for every 300 borrowed.[10]

About this time, the Mansa also learned that many of Cairo's merchants, believing the people of Mali to be naïve, had been charging them inflated prices. Therefore, when his Chief Steward went back out to finish buying their supplies, it was with strict orders to bargain hard and buy quickly.

Chapter 13
AN ARDUOUS JOURNEY

AFTER LEAVING CAIRO, THE CARAVAN SIMPLY AND STEADILY WALKED OUT INTO THE DESERT. When Cairo was no longer visible, even as a speck in the distance, the immensity of the desert closed down upon them. Hot, dry, barren, vast, lonely, and dangerous, the huge Sahara stretched before them once again.

By now, each member of the caravan was aware of the difficulties that lay ahead. For some, the incredible heat during the summer months was the hardest to bear; for others, it was when the wind became filled with tons of dust or sand and they could only bend before it and endure. For the Mansa, it was the monotony and apparent endlessness of this empty land. For his senior wife, Ināri Kunāte, it was the constant layer of grime and dust that penetrated her clothing and clung to her skin.

*One evening, back when they were crossing the Sahara for the first time, Ināri had felt that she just couldn't bear the

---

* This remarkable story has been told and retold for almost 700 years.

dirt and grime any longer. So, that night she turned to her husband and moaned, "Kankan, I am weary, and I can't sleep. My body is covered with dust and grime. How I wish I could splash about and swim carefree in the river as I did at home."

Secretly, the Mansa summoned his head servant, Farba, to his tent and told him of Inari's wish. "Always," Kankan said, "I've been able to give her everything she's wished for, but only Allah could create a river in this barren place."

Bowing low and beating his chest, Farba exclaimed, "May Allah the All-Merciful grant your wish!" Then he hurried outside, gathered his men and told them to dig a trench along a thousand foot line. As the men dug, a wall was thrown up that was three times the height of a man. Next, the trench was lined with gravel and packed with sand for its entire length. On top of the sand, the men placed blocks of wood which were then rubbed with the oil of kharite nuts. One touch of a flaming torch and the melting oil filled in every crevice to form a smooth channel. Thousands of servants were sent to an oasis for water, and in a short time the huge canal was filled with gently rolling waves. A miniature river had sprung up in the desert!

Just as the sun began to rise, Ināri and her 500 women were led in silence to the canal. Shrieks of joy and astonishment broke the morning's stillness as the laughing, unbelieving women ran and plunged into the water.[II]

When the caravan re-entered the Sahara to begin its long trip back across the desert, the Mansa decided not to allow any unnecessary stops. While he could easily eliminate these delays, the slow pace of the caravan was becoming more and more difficult for him to bear. In his frustration, he began to order it forward with increasing impatience. Yet, no matter how impatient he became or how efficiently his staff worked and planned, a caravan consisting of tens of thousands of people traveling by foot can only go so fast.

The addax, a species of antelope that lives in the driest parts of the Sahara, can live its whole life without ever having a drink of water. Adult males weigh up to 420 pounds.

About this time, far to the south of the caravan, a hard-riding messenger left the city of Gao with news that would radically change the Mansa's plans. The messenger knew the Mansa's intended route; he also knew that neither a caravan's route nor its schedule could be followed precisely when crossing the Sahara. So, for almost a thousand miles, he rode hard both day and night, stopping to sleep only when necessary. Then, when he reached the area where he thought he'd find the Mansa's caravan, he rode only by day, carefully scanning the horizon every few minutes. Finally, far out across the empty landscape, he saw a huge caravan.

Rushed directly to the Mansa, the exhausted messenger respectfully prostrated himself before his emperor. Then, in short, breathless phrases, he announced his exciting news. "Your Majesty, Gao has been captured! The Songhai army has been defeated! The King of Songhai is ready to surrender!"

While listening to the messenger's news, the Mansa's old love of military conquest surged within him. He felt once again the thrill his early victories had given him. During the years before his pilgrimage, he had been proud of his reputation as a great military leader. His successful strategies and his powerful, highly disciplined army had added many lands to Mali's empire. Now, in his absence, his army had defeated the Songhai in what was probably their greatest victory. It meant vast tracts of land and two great cities would be added to Mali's empire. Although overjoyed by the messenger's news, the Mansa was suddenly seized by an overwhelming desire to play an important role in this great victory. That evening, he summoned the caravan's lead guide. "Take us south to Gao," he told the surprised guide.

Then, seeking out his friend the Moor, the Mansa proudly explained the change in plans. "My army has defeated the Songhai in battle. All the Songhai lands, their important cities and much of their wealth will soon belong to Mali. I have decided to delay our return to Niani so that I can receive the King of Songhai's statement of submission myself! Also, although I will allow the Songhai to run their own internal affairs, I will establish Mali's control over their military forces, their foreign affairs, and set the amount and terms of their tribute. Then, after touring Gao and concluding any other business I may have there, we will resume our journey to Niani."

Chapter 14
A GREAT ACQUISITION

DRESSED IN HIS MOST REGAL ATTIRE AND MOUNTED on a handsome black stallion that had been lavishly adorned with gold, the Mansa made his triumphant entrance into the city of Gao. Soon he would meet the once powerful King of Songhai, dictate the terms of peace, and claim Gao and all the Songhai lands for Mali. Proud of his role, his army and his splendid caravan, the majestic Emperor of Mali rode into Gao.

For the recently defeated people of Gao, the very sight of Mansa Musa and his enormous caravan, still spectacular and glittering with gold and jewels, was overwhelming. They stared, suddenly fully aware of the consequences of their defeat. Mansa Musa's power and great wealth were brutally apparent. They knew that he had come to dictate the terms of their surrender and that he could enforce any terms he chose. They knew that his empire stretched west for hundreds of miles, clear to a distant ocean, and that it reached far into the Sahara to the north and the equatorial forests to the south. They knew it included their city now, and their lands, too.

71

As well as being a most impressive figure, the Mansa was a masterful diplomat. His meeting with the King of Songhai, for instance, was carefully orchestrated so that each ruler received the honor due him. After the initial ceremonies, the Mansa listened quietly to the king's statement of submission and in all ways treated him with respect. The terms of his peace agreement were fair, given the standards of his day, and the amount of tribute demanded was generally considered just, given the great wealth of the Songhai Kingdom.

Shrewd as well as diplomatic, the Mansa decided to take the Songhai king's two sons back to Niani with him as guest-hostages. They would be employed as officers in Mali's army and would be well-treated, but their whereabouts would be closely monitored and they would not be allowed to leave Mali. The Mansa did this to help ensure that the Songhai king would keep the terms of his surrender and to create a measure of Songhai loyalty toward Mali's rule.

As a result of their defeat, many of the Songhai people were forced into servitude. They were sent to work in Mali's mines, to grow food for Mali's army, to establish new villages for Mali's empire, or to work as personal servants for Mali's elite. The Mansa alone had thousands of "slaves." Most of them served him and, at the same time, Mali's government. Some held highly skilled and responsible positions: provincial governors, for example, were often slaves. Though powerful, they were dependent upon the emperor and could not make a competing claim to the throne as a member of the emperor's family might. Although these people had been defeated in battle and forced into servitude, they could choose to save their wages and buy back their freedom. They could socialize with, and even marry, anyone in Mali. Perhaps because everyone knew that any free person could be forced into servitude if captured in war, and that through hard work slaves could become free, these people weren't treated as chattel. Even though Mali had won many victories, the proportion of these servant-slaves, relative to the rest of the population, remained small.

While still in Gao, the Mansa toured the city. Its bustling trade and the great expanse of its lands delighted him, but when he saw the straw-roofed mud hut that served as the mosque for this great city, he was dismayed. Calling the Moor to him, he asked his friend to build a mosque whose magnificence would make it a suitable place in which to praise the never-ending glory of Allah.

The handsome mosque the Mansa commissioned the Moor to build in Gao introduced Mali and the rest of the Sudan to a new style of architecture, a style that became known as the Malian style of architecture. Built of sun-dried bricks, another advance introduced by the Mansa and the Moor, Gao's tall and graceful mosque was greatly admired for hundreds of years.

After leaving Gao, the caravan followed the Niger River to Timbuktu, another large and important Songhai city that now belonged to Mali. The Mansa was thrilled with the city, its location, and its busy commercial center. Timbuktu was the most important of the northern port cities because, in addition to long caravans of camels and donkeys, hundreds upon hundreds of canoes carried goods into and out of Timbuktu.

For 1000 miles, from Timbuktu in the north to the heart of Mali's empire in the south, canoes carried goods and people up and down the Upper Niger. Long, up to 66 feet in length, needle-nosed and wonderfully graceful, these sturdy, handmade canoes carried up to a ton and a half of cargo. They were flat-bottomed for stability and

This is a photo of a mosque in Mali that exemplifies the style of architecture introduced by Mansa Musa and As-Sāhilī. The boards sticking out of the sides of the building (called toron) are for people to climb up and stand on while replastering. During replastering, which is done at the end of each year's rainy season, cured mud is rubbed by hand over the entire exterior of the structure to repair any rain damage. After being replastered, the building looks like new and if maintained in this simple way it will last for centuries. (Ladders are used when replastering smaller structures like people's homes.)

good maneuverability even in very shallow water. Many of the larger canoes had arched roofs made of boughs covered with thatch.

All of this delighted the Mansa, but, once again, he was dismayed when he saw the small building that served as the city's mosque. So, he sent a message back to Gao commissioning the Moor to build a new mosque in Timbuktu, also. When it was finished, Timbuktu's large and strikingly handsome mosque became the early home of the University of Sankoré. Founded and supported during its early years by Mansa Musa, the University of Sankoré became a renowned university where thousands of talented black African scholars taught beside and studied with scholars from Europe, Asia and North Africa.

Chapter 15

WELCOME HOME

SOON AFTER HIS ARRIVAL IN TIMBUKTU, the Mansa ordered several barges built so that he and Ināri, the other women, and the *shurafā* could ride from Timbuktu to Niani in comfort. The rest of the caravan would continue on by land. So, when his business in Timbuktu was finished, the Mansa and his fellow passengers stepped aboard the newly completed barges and began their leisurely journey up the Niger River to Niani.

By the time the barges approached Niani, a spirited celebration was already under way. Groups of skilled musicians were playing lively music. Scores of chefs were busy preparing an extravaganza

12

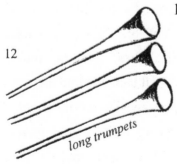

long trumpets

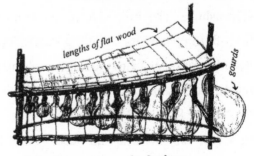

lengths of flat wood

gourds

balaphon – a type of xylophone

77

gold and silver guimbris two-stringed guitars

leather calabash

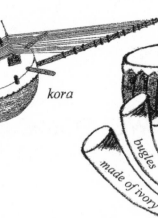

kora

bugles made of ivory

drums

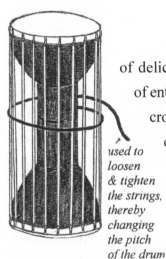

used to loosen & tighten the strings, thereby changing the pitch of the drum

talking drum

of delicious foods, enough for everyone. Dozens of entertainers were dancing and juggling, but the crowds around them kept shrinking as people drifted down to the river's edge in the hope of seeing Mansa Musa's arrival.

"There he is!" "He's back!" "The Mansa is back!" The crowd cheered and shouted, eager to welcome him back and to celebrate his safe return. When the barges finally landed, the huge crowd parted to let the Mansa and his fellow passengers step ashore. The mix of brightly colored clothes, pounding music, high-flying pennants, cheering voices, colorful banners, and the wonderful fragrances from the huge cooking pots swirled wildly about as the entire city did its best to welcome home its well-loved emperor.

Mansa Kankan Musa, the Emperor of Mali, was home! His days in Mecca and Medina had been wonderful. The large addition to the empire had been an unexpected thrill. His journey, though long and difficult, had at times been fascinating. Someday he hoped to return to Mecca, but for now he was just glad to be home. Looking about happily, he smiled and greeted the large crowd, then eagerly walked forward to see his son Maghan, who had been left behind to serve as Mali's emperor during his absence.

In the days that followed, the Mansa spent many hours talking with Maghan, his governors, and his senior military officers. Slowly, and with great sorrow, he discovered that the reports indicating that Maghan was a weak leader were true. As he learned about his son's lack of ability, his own dream of returning to Mecca to live out his life in study and prayer faded, and finally died away completely. He knew now that he couldn't leave Mali. In fact, he was worried about Mali's future, knowing that when he died, Maghan would become the Emperor of Mali. By then, perhaps, Maghan would be stronger and more capable. He certainly hoped so.

By this time, the Empire of Mali was the second largest empire or kingdom in the world. It was composed of a vast collection of individual villages, cities, provinces, and states. Each village had a chief. Important cities were governed by an inspector (or mayor). The provinces, which were made up largely of Mali's core population, the Mandingo people, were ruled by governors. The states, which were lands that had been conquered by Mali's troops, were generally ruled by their own leaders if these leaders swore allegiance to Mali, supplied troops when requested, and paid tribute to the empire. Even when compliant, local leaders were sometimes supervised by a resident representative of the emperor. A large, paid bureaucracy ran the complex political machinery that maintained Mali's system of law and order.

Each governor, supervisor, city leader, high-ranking military officer, top bureaucrat, and foreign diplomat reported directly and personally to the emperor himself. To maintain control, peace, and prosperity throughout the empire required a leader with a strong personality and great skill. The Mansa was such a man. Maghan was not, at least not yet.

Chapter 16
MALI'S GOLDEN AGE

Mansa Musa continued to serve as Mali's emperor until his death in 1337. During these years, the Empire of Mali reached its greatest heights in terms of size, wealth, power, stability, culture, and general prosperity.

ONCE HE DECIDED TO STAY IN MALI, the Mansa began to focus much of his energy on the projects he'd been dreaming about ever since talking with the scholars in Mecca. Still other plans grew out of the impact Cairo had made on him. One of the first projects he carried out was to commission the Moor to build more mosques and several new palaces. Each newly completed building became another exciting example of the Malian style of architecture he had first introduced in Gao.

The royal palace the Moor built in Timbuktu, for instance, was a large, square-cornered, stone structure, quite unlike the rounded clay buildings Mali's people were used to seeing. It had an airy porch, a soaring cupola, and plaster walls that were decorated with intricate designs painted in flaming colors. Both tourists and townspeople came to see it, admire its style, and enjoy its colorful frescoes.

During these years, the Mansa became an increasingly ardent patron of the sciences and the arts, Islamic religious studies, history and the law. In Timbuktu alone, where he founded the University of Sankoré, he supported, very handsomely, many of the scholars, judges, doctors, clerics and other learned men who gathered there to teach and to study.

As the university grew, so did the profits of the city's book traders. By the time the University of Sankoré was well established, Timbuktu's book traders were making larger profits than any of the city's other merchants, even those trading in ivory, copper or gold! In addition to purchasing books, the university's scholars wrote a great many books: histories and biographies, collections of poetry, books of science and medicine, and countless volumes of both legal and religious essays. Some of their work is still being read in Koranic[*] schools today.

Though smaller, the other mosques the Mansa commissioned also became centers of education as well as of prayer. In them, lessons and prayers were conducted in Arabic, the scholarly language that was used in Mali and throughout most of the Muslim world, much as Latin was used across most of Western Europe. As Mali's empire grew, its government became increasingly sophisticated and its populace more literate.

The Mansa and his pilgrimage ushered in a new era of increased contact with Egypt and, through Egypt, other Arab and European countries. New embassies were established which became actively engaged in diplomatic relations with other nations. Cultural exchanges with other countries became more frequent. Foreign trade increased in volume. During this time, Mali's major cities became important

---

[*] Koranic schools provide boys and girls with an Islamic education, i.e., their curriculum includes Islamic religious education courses.

metropolitan centers of commerce and culture. These were the empire's greatest years—the heart of its Golden Age.

Mansa Musa's pilgrimage startled the world by suddenly introducing it to a vast and powerful empire, an empire that almost no one beyond the Sudan had even heard of. This immense empire was about the same size as all the lands of Western Europe combined, and its wealth, in terms of gold, was beyond imagining. Almost overnight, Mali was recognized as a world power. It also became the talk of the world's adventurers, merchants and financiers. Mysterious and enticing, this vast "golden" land beckoned to them and to all who wanted or needed gold, adventure, and riches.

Although the Mansa did not foresee the consequences of announcing the existence of Mali's stupendous supply of gold to the whole world, he did fully comprehend both the importance of the gold trade to Mali's economy and the need to keep its source a secret.

a gold plant

Therefore, when someone he wanted to be polite to, such as the Sultan of Egypt, pressed him to tell them how to reach the source of Mali's gold, the Mansa had a story he liked to tell.[13] The story was amusing, yet, as it unfolded his listener learned, in a pleasant way, that the subject should be dropped.

"In a distant corner of my empire," the Mansa would begin, "gold grows from the ground on plants and is picked like grain. Only the people who inhabit this far-off land know how to cultivate gold plants properly. These distant people have a strange power over their plants," the Mansa would add with a smile, "that protects them from outsiders. You see, if anyone tries to steal one of their gold plants, or even just pick a bit of gold from one of them, the plant will suddenly wither and die.

"So, even though these people are among Mali's subjects and pay Mali a handsome tribute in pure gold, they must be left in peace; otherwise, the golden harvest will end!"

During Mansa Musa's reign, the golden harvest did not end. Instead, it grew and blossomed most wonderfully. Very early in his reign, he had learned that it was best to leave the gold miners in peace and that it was important to rid the land of bandits. As a result, the flow of gold into and through Mali grew. Throughout his long reign, the Mansa continued to foster, protect, and tax the immensely lucrative gold trade that formed the basis of Mali's economic prosperity.

Chapter 17
NOT BY GOLD ALONE

GOLD WAS THE FOUNDATION OF MALI'S PROSPERITY, but gold alone did not lift Mali into its Golden Age. The gold trade had been

the basis of the Empire of Ghana's prosperity for hundreds of years, long before the Empire of Mali superseded it. The method used to mine the gold was an old, completely indigenous technology. The main trading routes and the practice of taxing the gold trade were also centuries old. So, although gold was the basis of Mali's prosperity, it wasn't until Mansa Musa—with his vision, personal strength, superb administrative skills and military expertise—became emperor that Mali entered its Golden Age.

Under his leadership, Mali's agricultural production was expanded and

Though best known for its gold, Mali also exported a lot of copper. By the 1000s in Ife and the 1300s in Benin, Mali's copper was being used by highly skilled artists to create beautiful bronze sculptures. The above drawing is of a bronze sculpture of an ancient queen mother.[14]

diversified to create a solid base for the empire's tremendous growth. In addition, throughout the entire empire, the Mansa established a single, highly effective system of law and order; oversaw a system of taxation that allowed both individual traders and Mali's government to prosper; established a military presence that provided peace and stability across hundreds of thousands of square miles; and oversaw an efficient system of trade that provided Mali with a plentiful and diverse supply of goods. These complex, well-organized systems provided Mali's people with a standard of living that was, in terms of food, personal safety, and freedom, comparable to or better than that found in contemporary Europe.[15]

Mansa Musa also left a legacy of cultural and religious values that endured long after his death. Ridding the land of bandits had, in addition to all its economic benefits, expanded people's horizons. Their marketplaces became living encyclopedias of the world where silks and knives and cinnamon were displayed beside ivory, drums, copper and cattle—all of which was sold to the accompaniment of lively music, news of the world, and exciting tales of adventure. Foreign diplomats, travelers, merchants, entertainers, scholars, and traders visited Mali's cities in complete safety. The University of Sankoré, which the Mansa founded, continued to grow in size and status. Stately mosques stood as examples of architectural innovation and as centers of education and public prayer. Mali's principal cities became cosmopolitan centers of commerce and culture, and its countryside peaceful and prosperous.

It was a time of glory, a time to remember.

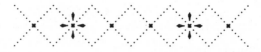

How do we know so much about Mansa Musa and the Empire of Mali? Historians, scholars and Mali's great epic chronicle the history of Mali and its empire. Thousands of texts written by African scholars in Timbuktu that preserve the traditions of Mali still exist.[16] The vividly descriptive memoirs written during Mali's Golden Age by al-'Umari and other authors are, according to a modern expert, as good as anything we have from medieval Europe.[17] Mansa Musa had secretaries and offices, merchants kept records, judges and scholars wrote letters, books, and treatises. Archaeologists continue to make discoveries. All of these sources have contributed to our considerable, though still incomplete, knowledge of Mali's Golden Age.

Even today, singers and poets delight audiences in Mali by reciting the *Epic of Old Mali*. Long ago, each new *dyeli* memorized the epic and added to it the story of his own times. Thus, over time, the epic grew. Crowds of people listened to the *dyelis* recitations and remembered the epic's lyrical and rhythmic words. When there were no more *dyelis*, each generation told the next the story of those golden years when the Empire of Mali had spread so far across the land, when food was plentiful, and the army was strong and victorious. They told how great scholars had come from distant lands to study, of imported silks and richly decorated brocades. It was a glorious time, they said, when Mali's cities were known for their culture, when gold was abundant, and peace and prosperity prevailed across their land.

EPILOGUE

DURING MAGHAN'S SHORT REIGN, Timbuktu was captured and burned by the Mossi people. The two Songhai princes escaped and returned to Gao, where one of the brothers established himself as king in his father's old palace. In time, the Songhai people drove Mali's officials from their land and successfully refused to pay further tribute to Mali. The new Songhai Kingdom continued to grow stronger until it replaced the Empire of Mali as the dominant political force in West Africa.

After only four years as emperor, Maghan Musa died. Mansa Musa's brother, Sulayman Musa, became Mali's next emperor. He was not a gifted leader like Mansa Musa, nor was he as well-liked, but he was competent and he ruled successfully for many years. At the end of his reign, Mali's Golden Age ended.

GLOSSARY

Abu Bakari II – Known as "the Voyager King," he was Mansa Musa's uncle and his predecessor to the throne of Mali.

Abu Ishāq as-Sāhilī – Often referred to as "the Moor," he was a poet and architect from Granada whom Mansa Musa met in Mecca and persuaded to return to Mali with him. The mosques and palaces the Mansa commissioned As-Sāhilī to build introduced new methods of building and a new style of architecture to the Sudan.

Abu'l 'Abbas Ahmed ben Abil'l Haki, el Mehmendar – The Egyptian official who, on behalf of the Sultan of Egypt, went out to greet Mansa Musa when he entered Cairo.

Ali Koleni – One of the two Songhai princes taken to Mali as guest-hostages by Mansa Musa after Mali's forces defeated the Songhai in battle. In Mali, Ali Koleni became a soldier and was highly regarded for his leadership ability. While working in this capacity, he secretly began to stockpile supplies and weapons along the route from Niani to Gao. Then, shortly after

Mansa Musa's death, he and his brother escaped and returned to Gao where Ali Koleni established himself as Songhai's king.

Allah – The Arabic word for God.

Arabian horse – Any of a breed of horses originally raised in Arabia and known for their endurance, elegance, speed and intelligence. Gray, a whole range of shades, is the most common color for Arabian horses; but there are also chestnut, bay, sorrel and occasionally white or black Arabian horses.

Baobab tree – A large, useful tree that grows wild in the grasslands of West Africa.

Cairo – The large, vibrant, Egyptian city that Mansa Musa stayed in on his way to and from Mecca. Ibn Khaldun praised it, calling it "the metropolis of the universe."

Canoes and Ships – Long before the advent of saws, West African boat-builders began making canoes. In the forests of what is now Guinea, these ingenious boat-builders felled trees by burning through the base of a tree's trunk until it crashed to the ground. The downed trees were stripped and made into dugouts right where they fell. When finished, the heavy canoes were manhandled to the nearest waterway and launched.

Today, and for the last thousand years or so, canoes are made from boards sent downriver from the forests in Guinea to villages along the banks of the lower Upper Niger River. Carefully measured, cut, and shaped, the hand-hewn boards are fastened together with spikes the boat-builders make

92

Photos were taken by Omer MEKAYI in 2007.

themselves. The resulting sleek, flat-bottomed canoes are used by fishermen, farmers, traders, and transporters all along the Upper Niger and throughout Mali's huge inland delta.

For hundreds of years, the fishermen of Dakar have wrestled their boats (large seafaring vessels built with heavy planks cut from the giants of the rainforest) through the ocean's surf to the smoother waters beyond, just as Mansa Musa's uncle's men must have done. From Dakar, which is almost certainly the place his uncle's fleet departed from,[18] the prevailing winds blow toward the west and the ocean's currents flow to the west. All Abu Bakari II and his men needed to do to reach the New World was to stay afloat long enough—any paddling they did or sails they might have used, would only have served to shorten their time at sea.[19]

Cavalry – An armed force whose members are mounted on horseback.

Citadel in Cairo – The Citadel was a large stone fortress that encircled the Sultan's Palace, the Mosque of an-Nasir (which was being built when Mansa Musa was in Cairo), the headquarters of the Sultan's government and of his army, barracks for many of his soldiers, housing for his harem and courtiers, wells, kitchens, etc. According to legend, the location of the Citadel complex was chosen in part for its "good air." Saladin—the ruler of Egypt then—ordered pieces of meat hung in a variety of places around the capital. The pieces that were hung on the Muqattam Hills stayed fresh the longest, so he decided to build the Citadel there.

Cresques, Abraham – A Majorcan cartographer who, in 1375, completed his masterpiece, the Catalan Atlas, for Charles V of France. It included a map of Mali and a drawing of Mansa Musa.

Dyeli – Each emperor of Mali had a dyeli who served as his herald and spokesman, counselor, and intimate friend—he was the only person, for instance, allowed to see the emperor in his wrath. He recited the *Epic of Old Mali* in public, composed the portion of the epic that related the events occurring during his time as dyeli, and served as the court's master of ceremonies. Trained in constitutional procedures, he also settled disputes between clans and tribes.

Dyelis were chosen, in part, because of their low social status. This was considered important because it meant the *dyelis* would be dependent upon "their" emperor and would not have any kinsmen among the nobility or the freemen who might try to influence them or make a claim to the throne. For these reasons, though the *dyelis* held a very important position in Mali's government, it was believed they were reliable.

Empire of Ghana – The first of the three great empires of West Africa (700 – 1200 A.D.).

Empire of Mali – The second of the three great empires of West Africa (1200 – 1500 A.D.).

Empire of Songhai – The third of the three great empires of West Africa (1350 – 1600 A.D.).

Gao – The capital city of the Songhai peoples. Defeated by Mali's forces in 1325, Gao became one of Mali's great commercial centers.

Guimbris – Two-stringed, gold and silver guitars that were played in ancient Mali.

Hajj / hadj / haj – A Muslim's pilgrimage to Mecca.

Hajji / hadji / haj – A Muslim who has completed a pilgrimage to Mecca.

Hegira – The flight of Muhammad from Mecca to Medina in 622 A.D. This event marks the first year of the Muslim calendar.

Ibn – Means "the son of."

Ibn Battuta – Muhammad ibn Abdullah ibn Battuta (1304 – 1368/69) was a world famous traveler (75,000 miles by foot, camel, horse, and ship) and the author of one of the world's most famous travel books. He visited the Empire of Mali in 1352-53.

Ibn Khaldun – The greatest of the Arab historians (1332 – 1406), he wrote a chronicle of the empires of the Western Sudan using information he gathered from written records, interviews and, importantly, from the oral traditions of many different Sudanese peoples. Because Ibn Khaldun, alone among the Arab writers, included information from the oral traditions, he was better able to connect specific events and place them in context. According to Nehemia Levtzion (*Ancient Ghana and Mali*), this allowed him to write a history of West Africa's great empires that moved across the centuries in a dynamic, living way. His work is, therefore, an important link between the written records and the oral traditions of West Africa.

Ināri Kunāte – Mansa Musa's senior wife. She accompanied him on his pilgrimage to Mecca.

Islam – The world religion founded by the Prophet Muhammad.

Kaaba / Ka'ba / Ka'bah – The Islamic shrine in Mecca that contains the Sacred Black Stone.

King Assibai – The Songhai king whom Mali's forces defeated and from whom Mansa Musa received a statement of submission.

Kola nuts – Gathered from the kola trees that grew wild in the equatorial forests of southern West Africa, kola nuts were a valuable export during the Middle Ages. They are rich in stimulating alkaloids such as caffeine and have a bitter taste that relieves thirst. Highly prized in Arab communities, they were an important symbol of hospitality throughout the Sahel, the Sahara, North Africa and beyond. As with gold, Mali benefited financially from its role as middleman in the kola nut trade.

By the late 1900s, kola nuts had found their way around the world as an ingredient in Coca-Cola. However, the 1998 Encyclopedia Britannica states that "American and European soft-drink manufacturers do not use the kola nut; instead, they manufacture synthetic chemicals that resemble the flavour of the kola nut."

Koran / Qur'an – The Muslim holy book. It is revered as the Word of God and accepted by Muslims as the foundation of Islamic culture, law, commerce, political practices and religious beliefs.

Koranic schools – Traditionally, a first school for children in Islamic societies. The school teaches reading, writing, and sometimes arithmetic, but its emphasis is on studying and memorizing the Koran. In order to complete the school's curriculum, a child must memorize the entire Koran.

Lahote, Henri – A French explorer and ethnologist who, in 1956, discovered the Tassili n' Ajjer rock paintings and oversaw a group of artists who spent 16 months camped atop the Tassili Plateau meticulously reproducing the rock paintings.

Mandingo / Mandinka / Malinke – The founders and core population of the Empire of Mali.

Mansa – A Sudanese word meaning "emperor." It is sometimes translated as "king" or "sultan."

Mansa Kankan Musa – The Empire of Mali's greatest and most famous emperor. He ruled for 25 years from 1307 – 1332 (or 1312 - 1337).

Mansa Maghan – Mansa Musa's son and his successor to the throne of Mali.

Mansa Sulayman – Mansa Musa's brother. He became the Emperor of Mali following the death, often thought to be the result of foul play, of Mansa Maghan.

Mecca / Makkah – The holy city of Islam. Mecca is the destination of all Muslim pilgrims and the place toward which Muslims face when they pray. It is the site of the Kaaba, the Mount of Mercy, and other important religious sites.

Medina / Madinah – The city's name means "City of the Prophet." Muhammad fled to, governed, and gained a large following in Medina. Most pilgrims include a visit to Medina, which is located only 250 or so miles from Mecca, and its famous Mosque of the Prophet in their pilgrimage plans.

Moor – A member of a Muslim people of mixed Berber and Arab descent. During the time of Mansa Musa, there were many Moors, like his friend As-Sāhilī, living in Spain.

Mosque – An Islamic place of public worship.

Mosque of Sankoré – The mosque Mansa Musa commissioned As-Sāhilī to build in Timbuktu. It became the first home of the University of Sankoré.

Mud Architecture – There are only three standard methods of building with mud—*pisé de terre*, coursing or puddling, and building with sun-dried mud bricks—but there are a great many architectural styles used.

One and a half billion[20] of the world's people live in houses made of mud. Stretching from the high deserts of China, through India, Pakistan, and Afghanistan, across the Middle East and west across the great Sahara and Sahel of Africa is

A stylish red mud house in Mali

A small mosque in Mali

Small huts connected so as to create a communal courtyard and protective exterior wall

An ivory-colored mud house in Mali

an enormous expanse of very dry land. After leaping over the Atlantic, this huge crescent-shaped swath of desert continues on across northern Mexico and into the United States' Southwest.

The walls of a well-built mud house are thick, up to two feet thick. During a long, scorchingly hot day, the interior of the house stays cool because it takes so many hours for the sun's heat to penetrate the thick walls. At night, when the thin desert air becomes cold, the now thoroughly warm walls slowly release their heat into the home. So, although the temperature outside the home swings wildly, the temperature inside the house remains "remarkably constant."[21]

The Great Mosque of Djenné is the largest and most famous mud building in existence. Its construction features two spiral staircases that reach from the ground to the roof (about 40 feet), over one hundred equally tall columns, three massive towers, and tremendous, thick, side walls—all of which are made of mud. Thousands of sun-dried bricks, tons of thick mud for mortar, hundreds of gallons of finer mud for plastering, and very fine mud (clay) to make kiln fired items such as drainage pipes were used to construct this immense mosque.

Muhammad – The founder of Islam.

Muslim – A believer in Islam. The word means "one who surrenders to God."

Nasir, al-Malik an- / An-Nasir Muhammad/Al-Nasir Muhammad – The Sultan of Egypt whom Mansa Musa met in Cairo. He is remembered as one of the greatest of the Mamluk sultans.

Niani – The capital of the Empire of Mali and an important cultural and commercial center. It was close to the early gold fields, had the fertile plains of the Sankari River as its agricultural base, and enough iron ore in its soil to supply a number of iron-smelting furnaces. In addition, the city was located deep within Mali on a site that was easy to defend.

Niger River – A long, important river that flowed through the heart of Mali's Empire. It was the principal artery of Mali's east-west trade and communication systems and was vital to the empire's agricultural and fishing interests. Long ago, this almost horse-shoe-shaped river was, in fact, two rivers. One river flowed north and east into the Sahara; its upper portion probably traveled along much the same route as the upper portion of the Niger River does today. (This river emptied into a lake that, when it evaporated, created a great salt mine.) The other river originated in the Sahara and flowed south and west; its lower portion traveling along much the same route as the lower Niger does today. When the Sahara dried up, the two rivers merged creating a great inland delta that covers nearly 12,000 square miles.

For half the year the delta area is basically a "flat, featureless, treeless, grassless plain baking in the noonday sun."[22] Then, just before the floodwaters arrive, farmers plant hundreds of acres of rice on the flat delta land. As the slow moving floodwaters rise, the rice grows and matures. When the rice is mature, the farmers paddle out in their canoes to harvest it. Fish that have lain semi-dormant for six months somewhere in a narrow river channel or an isolated pond suddenly spring to life when the nutrient-rich flood waters reach them. Gulping down great quantities of food, they grow rapidly and spawn. In just two days most of their eggs hatch and their young, millions of them, join in the feeding craze. Then, when the floodwaters begin to recede, men, large carnivorous fish, and thousands upon thousands of birds flock to the delta to fish. A recent study states that in a typical year the inland delta's 50,000 fishermen sell 99,000 tons of fish.[23]

Sagmandia / Sagaman-dir – Mansa Musa's general. Under his direction, Mali's forces defeated the Songhai.

Sahara – Derived from the Arabic word for desert, our word Sahara also means desert. Therefore, the world's largest desert is most correctly called the Sahara, and not the Sahara Desert. The Sahara stretches all the way across Africa from the Atlantic Ocean to the Red Sea and covers an area about the size of the entire United States of America.

Interestingly, 7,000 years ago the Sahara was lush and green. Before that, 15,000 years ago, it was drier than it is today and 25,000 years ago wetter than it was only 7,000 years ago. These huge, slow, recurring changes in the Sahara's climate are due to long-term, cyclical variations in the Earth's orbit, tilt, and the precession of the equinoxes. These oscillations have been going on for millions of years.[24]

Amazingly, some of the guides who led caravans across the Sahara were blind. Unlike most guides, they depended upon the feel of the sun upon their face, their sense of smell, and perhaps the presence of a tuft of grass. Leo Africanus writes about a caravan that was "saved by a blind guide who 'riding foremost on his camel, commanded some sand be given to him at every mile's end by the smell whereof he declared the situation of the place.'"[25] Ibn Batutta told of a similar event, as have several other writer-travelers.

For more information about blind guides, see Note 25.

Sahel – The Arabic word for the Sahel means shore. The Sahel is the northern, semiarid portion of the Sudan. It is the transitional zone between the Sahara to the north and the wetter, more humid grasslands to the south. It extends across Africa from the Atlantic Ocean in the west to the mountains of Ethiopia in the east.

Sarāj al-Dīn ibn al-Kuwayk – The Egyptian merchant who loaned Mansa Musa the gold he needed in order to purchase supplies for his caravan. The high interest rate Sarāj al-Dīn charged (700 dinars to be repaid for every 300 borrowed) seems at least somewhat more reasonable when the difficulties he faced collecting on such a loan are considered. First, he sent an agent to collect his money, but the agent decided to stay in Mali.

So, Sarāj al-Dīn and his son traveled across the Sahara from Cairo to Timbuktu where, unfortunately, Sarāj al-Dīn died. His son, after caring for his father, continued on to Niani, collected all that was due his father, both principal and interest, and returned to Cairo. There were, of course, many expenses as well as dangers inherent in making a trip across the Sahara. One source (*The Cambridge History of Africa*) states that one-third of the people and animals in Mansa Musa's caravan died by the time the caravan returned to Niani—and the Mansa's was a very large, well-provisioned and well-guarded caravan.

Savanna – The long band of grasslands just south of the Sahara that stretches from the Atlantic Ocean to the mountains at the eastern edge of the African continent. The northernmost portion of the savanna, the Sahel, is the driest. Along its southern edge, the savanna is bordered by the equatorial rainforest, where it can rain up to 96 inches a year.

Shurafā / Sharif / Sherif and other variant spellings – Descendants of the Prophet Muhammad.

Sinai Peninsula – An extremely arid, triangular peninsula linking NE Africa with SW Asia. It is located at the north end of the Red Sea.

Slave / servant / serf – With a change in time, place, or culture, the meaning of these words changes. In West Africa during Mansa Musa's time, according to Basil Davidson and other modern experts on African history, slaves were generally people who had been captured in battle. Some, like those who worked in the salt mines at Taghaza, had a very hard life. Others, who worked for individuals or within Mali's government, often lived lives of considerable comfort and responsibility. They could easily earn their freedom, mingle with and even marry the citizens of Mali. Since no one worked for money and land was owned in common, the lines between the different strata of society were quite blurred and people moved up and down the rungs of social power much more easily than in medieval Europe.[26]

The origin of the word slave is Slav, because in the early Middle Ages so many Slavs had been captured and enslaved.

Songhai / Songhay – The Songhai were conquered by Mansa Musa's forces in 1325. Later on, they asserted their independence and slowly became the core peoples of West Africa's third great commercial empire.

Sudan – The Sudan is a vast tract of open grasslands that extends across Africa from the Atlantic Ocean to the mountains of Ethiopia. Sudan and South Sudan are also the names of two countries in the northeastern part of Africa.

Sulayman Nar – One of the Songhai king's sons taken to Mali as guest-hostages by Mansa Musa. See Ali Koleni in this book's Glossary.

Sultan of Egypt – See Nasir, al-Malik an-.

Sundiata / Mari-Djata – Founder of the Empire of Mali. He is remembered in the oral traditions of West Africa as a "great hero figure" (J. D. Fage in *A History of West Africa*) and as "a powerful man of magic and enchantment" (Basil Davidson in *Africa In History*). Against tremendous odds, he was victorious in a great battle with the oppressive ruler Sumanguru, and turned a small chiefdom into an empire.

Taghaza – A small town in the Sahara where the salt mines controlled by the Empire of Mali were located. Long ago, the area around Taghaza was the site of a large lake. When the Sahara dried up, the lake's water evaporated leaving behind thousands of tons of salt.

Takedda – A busy "port" city located in the far-eastern portion of Mali's Empire. In addition to trade, the city was famous for its copper mines. Cast in people's homes, thousands of copper rods were produced and exported from Takedda each year.

Tassili n' Ajjer – A vast, rugged, arid plateau located in the central portion of the Sahara. Surrounded by thousands of square miles of harsh desert, Tassili n' Ajjer is the site of one of the world's greatest, and most beautiful, collections of prehistoric art. The Tassili paintings of a lush and green land full of life, juxtaposed with the barrenness of their present surroundings, clearly document the Sahara's most recent swing from lush and green to dry and desolate.

The radical changes in the Sahara's climate are not related to today's "global-warming" debate. Instead, long-term, cyclical variations in the Earth's tilt, orbit, and in the precession of its equinoxes cause huge, slow, recurring climatic changes. (Seven thousand years ago the Sahara was lush and green. Fifteen thousand years ago it was drier than it is today, and 25,000 years ago wetter than only 7,000 years ago, etc.[24]) These big, slow, climatic changes have been going on for millions of years. Thus, 8,000 years ago, Tassili artists were painting scenes of men in boats hunting hippos, while Europe was busy shrugging off the last vestiges of its latest Ice Age.

The Tassili paintings are from 8,000 to 2,000 years old—the most recent being the most primitive, as were the last cultures to leave the Sahara as it dried up. Most of the Tassili paintings are beautifully drawn and richly colored. Some are fanciful: for example, there are Dr. Seuss-like drawings; elongated, gracefully flowing, almost stick-like figures; even outer-space-like alien figures. Most of the paintings, however, are realistic drawings of animals, both wild and domestic, and the people the artists lived among. They include scenes of musical instruments and costumed groups of dancers, of fashionable women riding on bullocks, of judges presiding, warriors in chariots, women harvesting, hunters giving chase, and so much more. The paintings show us a great many different styles of dress, headgear, and hairdos. They show us, too, that blonde as well as dark-haired whites and brown as well as black-skinned blacks shared the Sahara during its most recent lush and green period.

Perhaps best of all, these often exquisite paintings give us a glimpse into the surprisingly complex lives of some of our very-long-ago ancestors.

For more, see *African Kingdoms,* pp. 43-57; *The Search for the Tassili Frescoes;* and Henri Lhote in this book's Glossary.

Timbuktu – At its height, Timbuktu was one of the wealthiest and most cultured cities in the world. Located just north of the Niger River's Great Bend, at the southern edge of the Sahara, the medieval city of Timbuktu became a great commercial center. Traders came from every direction with merchandise piled high on boats, camels, and donkeys. Merchants and artisans, fishermen and farmers, all prospered. Thousands of students and scholars were also drawn to Timbuktu by the city's famed university. Their books and manuscripts, tens of thousands of them, still exist. According to Henry Louis Gates, Jr., in *Wonders of the African World*, about ten thousand are housed in the Ahmed Baba Center's library and at least another 50,000 have been carefully squirreled away in dusty back rooms by proud members of some of Timbuktu's leading families. These proud people, and the exceptionally dry desert air of Timbuktu, have protected and preserved these precious old manuscripts for hundreds of years.

In 2008, the digitization of Timbuktu's collections of fragile, old manuscripts was begun. More than 300 manuscripts are now available online. See *The New York Times'* article "Project Digitizes Works From the Golden Age of Timbuktu".

Tribute – Payment in money or goods that is required of one country (or person) by a stronger country (or person).

Tsetse fly – When a tsetse fly feeds on the blood (its only food) of a wild animal whose bloodstream contains trypanosomes, single-celled parasites, the tsetse fly ingests the trypanosomes and becomes a "host" fly. As a host fly, it will release trypanosomes into the bloodstream of every person and animal it bites from then on. Trypanosomes cause sleeping sickness in people, a dreaded disease that is often fatal. Cattle, horses, and camels—most species of domesticated animals—will almost always die if bitten by a host fly. The donkeys the traders used to carry goods south to the edge of the equatorial forest, tsetse fly country, were seldom harmed because donkeys have a natural tolerance to tsetse-transmitted parasites, and because their "job" involved only brief, light, and intermittent exposure to the flies. Neither the wild animals the tsetse flies generally feed on, nor the tsetse flies themselves are harmed by having trypanosomes in their blood.

Tsetse flies are found in or near Africa's equatorial forests and savanna woodlands. They need a warm, humid, shady place in which to live and can't survive in open grasslands or heavily grazed areas. Since they can't fly far and need to eat almost every day, they also need an adequate supply of prey nearby.

'Umari, al- /al-Omari – Shihab ad-Din Ahmad ibn Fadl Allah al-'Umari (1301-1349), was a renowned Arab historian who wrote about Mansa Musa and the Empire of Mali.

University of Sankoré – Founded in Timbuktu by Mansa Musa, the University of Sankoré became renowned throughout the

Muslim world. Its scholars wrote about a broad range of subjects. Their topics included the sciences of astronomy, botany, and mathematics; Islamic thought and practices; proverbs; legal opinions; and historical accounts. For more, see Timbuktu in this book's Glossary.

Walata – A "port" city at the southern edge of the Sahara, Walata was a large commercial and cultural center. Following Mansa Musa's pilgrimage, however, Walata's importance began to decline as trade with Egypt, which was usually carried through Timbuktu, increased.

Wangara – The area, probably Bambuk and maybe Bure, too, where the gold mines were. Confusingly, the term is and was also used to refer to the gold-traders themselves.

AUTHOR'S NOTE

A YOUNG MAN FROM MALI SAT DOWN NEXT TO ME ON THE BUS: "You're writing a book about Mansa Musa? I didn't know anyone in America knew who he was. He was our Lincoln!"

The main events of Mansa Musa's life are in history's records. Two of the most renowned ancient scholars to write about Mansa Musa and the Empire of Mali, al-'Umari and Ibn Battuta, wrote in a very engaging and personal style that included bits of dialogue and detailed descriptions of events, places, and people. Al-'Umari, a highly regarded historian, carefully interviewed people and then wrote about what he'd learned. Ibn Battuta, a world traveler and the author of one of the most famous travel books ever written, visited Mali for a year during its Golden Age. His writing is a first-hand account of his experiences told with wit, energy, and, occasionally, a Muslim bias. Ibn Khaldun, the greatest of the Arab historians, wrote a chronicle of the empires of the Western Sudan using information he gathered from written records, interviews and, importantly, from the oral traditions of many different Sudanese peoples. Because he, alone among the Arab writers, included information from the oral traditions, he was

111

able to write a history that, according to Nehemia Levtzion (*Ancient Ghana and Mali*), moved across the centuries in a dynamic, living way. His work is, therefore, an important link between the written records and the oral traditions of West Africa. Other ancient scholars from West as well as North Africa wrote histories of West Africa. Many of their books and manuscripts, tens of thousands of them, languish unpublished, but safe, in dusty back rooms in Timbuktu. Many others have disappeared, but some have survived, been translated and published. Well-worn stories, modern archeological excavations, and the *Epic of Old Mali* tell us more.

From these sources, modern scholars have written their histories of West Africa, and from their books (listed in Bibliography) I have culled and synthesized the story of Mansa Kankan Musa, Mali's greatest emperor. Sometimes I've had to choose between sources or have combined the information they offer. For instance, in the beginning, I have Kankan Musa standing beside his uncle. His true relationship to this man is uncertain—sources vary. Was he his uncle, as some sources state, or a cousin perhaps? Historians agree that the "uncle" was a direct descendant of Sundiata, Kankan's great-uncle. Because matrilineal succession was still occasionally practiced in Mali, I chose to make him Kankan's uncle. Twice, when he is traveling north, I have attributed to Mansa Musa observations that were actually made by Ibn Battuta during his visit to Mali. In an effort to bring Mansa Musa and his society more fully to life, especially for young readers, I have added a few details such as the color of Mansa Musa's horse and bits of dialogue between the Mansa and his servant, but **always** this information is in keeping with the events and emotions described by the scholars listed in my Bibliography. A well-known children's biographer, Kathryn Lasky, calls this process "responsible imagining."

I have not written much about the women of Mali because the ancient scholars themselves wrote little about them. Basil Davidson, a modern expert on African history, gives two reasons for this lack of information in his book *African Civilization Revisited*. First, the writers were men. Secondly, the mutual respect between men and women recommended by Muhammad had been replaced by a "stiff male supremacism" in the countries of North Africa, and most of the ancient scholars who wrote about Mali were either from North Africa or were influenced by their traditions.

South of the Sahara this attitude of male supremacy was not admired or even acknowledged. For instance, when Ibn Battuta visited the home of a well-respected resident of Walata (*African Civilization Revisited*), he was deeply shocked to see his host's wife visiting with another man. "You permit this?" he asked. "Yes," his host replied, "the association of men and women is agreeable to us and a part of good manners."

I have enjoyed my journey to pre-colonial, sub-Saharan Africa and to the mighty Sahara. I hope you found your journey as interesting and as enjoyable as mine has been.

ACKNOWLEDGEMENTS

I WOULD LIKE TO EXPRESS MY APPRECIATION FOR THE INVALUABLE HELP OF THE FOLLOWING PEOPLE: Jenni James–a most skilled writer, David H. Copp–a computer wizard, Dorcas Abbot–a skilled and helpful librarian, California's interlibrary loan program, Marty Dunn and Catharine Gill for editorial help, Katharine Ball, Barbara White, Vista Pickett, Julian Grey and Linda Stephenson.

I would also like to acknowledge my indebtedness to a host of historians, archeologists, photographers, artists, dyelis and griots whose efforts have made the telling of this story possible. Also, and most importantly, I am indebted to the fascinating and courageous people of pre-colonial Africa who lived the lives that created the story I've told.

NOTES

Complete information for all sources cited here can be found in the Bibliography.

1) While in Cairo, Mansa Musa told Ibn Amir Hajib, a Cairene (person from Cairo) scholar, the story of his uncle's voyage and of his own succession to the throne. A few years later, Ibn Hajib repeated the Mansa's story to al-'Umari who included it in his book *Masalik ab Absar fi Mamalik al Amsar*. For more information, see *African Civilization Revisited: From Antiquity to Modern Times*, pp. 95-6; *Introduction To African Civilizations*, pp. 234-5, 261-2; *African Saga: a brief introduction to african history*, p.123; *General History of Africa·IV: Africa from the Twelfth to the Sixteenth Century*, pp. 150-1; *The Lost Cities of Africa*, pp. 74-5; *Wonders Of The African World*, p. 132; *The Story of Africa*, p. 113; "'Umari, al-." *Encyclopedia Britannica*, 15th Edition, 1998.

2) For evidence that supports the belief that West Africans arrived in the New World before Columbus, see *Introduction To African Civilizations*, pp. 232-263; *The African presence in Ancient America: They Came Before Columbus*, This book includes a good

collection of photos that support its premise that black Africans reached the Americas before Columbus. *The Story of Africa*, p.113. For more, see the Canoes and Ships entry in this book's Glossary.

3) *Africa: A Companion to the P B S Series*, p. 77; *The Cambridge History of Africa: Volume 3: from c. 1050 to c. 1600*, p. 283; *A History of Africa*, p. 90; *Africa Before the White Man*, p. 39; "kola nut." *Encyclopedia Britannica*, 15th Edition, 1998.

4) *The Cambridge History of Africa: Volume 3: from c. 1050 to c. 1600*, pp. 386-7; *Ancient Ghana and Mali*, pp. 111, 115-6, 148, 178; *The Lost Cities of Africa*, pp. 71-2, 80; *General History of Africa·IV: Africa from the Twelfth to the Sixteenth Century*, p. 164; *African Kingdoms*, pp. 30-1; *The Horizon History Of Africa*, pp. 210, 225; *A History of Africa*, pp. 71-2, 90; *Topics in West African History*, p. 7; *The Kingdoms of Africa*, p. 24; *Africa In History*, pp. 75-6.

5) *African Kingdoms*, pp. 89, 81-2; *A History of the African People*, pp. 64-7, 77; *History of West Africa*, pp. 142-3; *Ancient Ghana and Mali*, pp. 115-6, 123, 132, 148-9, 163, 179-81; *General History of Africa·IV: Africa from the Twelfth to the Sixteenth Century*, pp. 164-71; *The Story of Africa*, pp. 90-1.

6) *African Kingdoms*, pp. 43-57. This book contains an excellent collection of Tassili n' Ajjer paintings.

7) *The African Past*, p. 75; "Musa." *Encyclopedia Britannica*, 15th Edition, 1998; *The Golden Trade of the Moors*, p. 24; *African Saga*, p. 124.

8) "Fortress of the Mountain," *Saudi Aramco World*, March-April, 1993, pp. 32-9. http//www.saudiaramcoworld.com/issue/199302/ fortress.of.the.mountain.htm; *Cairo*, pp. 85-7; *Cairo: 5500 Years*, p. 92.

9) *The Lost Cities of Africa*, p. 72; *The Golden Trade of the Moors*, p. 114.

10) *Ancient Ghana and Mali*, pp. 212-3. For more information, see Sarāj al-Dīn ibn al-Kuwayk in this book's Glossary.

11) *Shapers of Africa*, pp. 25-6; *The Story of Africa*, pp. 110-1.

12) *Musical Instruments of Africa; Their Nature, Use, and Place in the Life of a Deeply Musical People*, pp. 24-39, 46, 64-5, 69, 83-5; *African Kingdoms*, pp. 27, 83; *African Saga*, p. 130; *The Kingdoms of Africa*, p. 26; *The Royal Kingdoms of Ghana, Mali, and Songha*i, p.73; "kora." Google Search, 2005.

13) *Shapers of Africa*, pp. 28-9.

14) *Africa's Glorious Legacy*, pp. 114, 116.

15) *A History of Africa*, p. 78; *The Lost Cities of Africa*, pp. 80-1, 90-1; *General History of Africa·IV: Africa from the Twelfth to the Sixteenth Century*, pp. 156, 165; *Introduction To African Civilizations*, pp. 211-2; *Africa In History*, p. 125; *Ancient African Kingdoms*, p. 56; *The Kingdoms of Africa*, p. 29.

16) *Wonders Of The African World*, pp. 144-5; *The New York Times*, "Project Digitizes Works From the Golden Age of Timbuktu" 20 May 2008. In 2008, a team from Northwestern University initiated

the digitization of these texts for the Internet and for distribution to scholars worldwide.

17) *The African Past: Chronicles from Antiquity to Modern Times*, p. 64.

18) *Into Africa: A Journey through the Ancient Empires*, p. 266.

19) *The Story of Africa*, p. 113.

20) *Spectacular Vernacular: The Adobe Tradition*, p. 41. This book contains an excellent selection of photographs of mud architecture.

21) Ibid., p. 56.

22) *Into Africa: A Journey Through the Ancient Empires*, p. 261; *Africa: A Companion to the P B S Series*, p. 191.

23) *Africa: A companion to the P B S Series*, p. 192.

24) *Africa: A companion to the P B S Series*. p. 64; *Africa: A Biography Of The Continent*, p. 37.

25) *The Golden Trade of the Moors*, pp. 92-3. This source refers to several accounts of blind Saharan guides. For more, see *The Christian Science Monitor*, "Salt of the earth and stars," 26 January 1983; *The History of the Long Captivity and Adventures of Thomas Pellow, in South-Barbary*, pp. 202-204.

26) *A History of West Africa: To The Nineteenth Century*, pp. 175-181; *Africa: History of a Continent*, p. 118.

BIBLIOGRAPHY

Ajayi, J.F.A., and Michael Crowder, editors. *History of West Africa*, vol.1. New York: Columbia University Press, 1976.

Amin, Mohamed. *Journey Of A Lifetime: Pilgrimage to Mekkah*. Nairobi: Camerapix Publishers International, 2000.

Boahen, Adu, with J.F. Ade Ajayi and Michael Tidy. *Topics in West African History*. Essex, England: Longman Group, 1986.

Bourgeois, Jean-Louis, with historical essay by Basil Davidson. *Spectacular Vernacular: The Adobe Tradition*. New York: Aperture Foundation, Inc., 1989.

Bovill, E.W. *The Golden Trade of the Moors*. London: Oxford University Press, 1958 & 1968 editions.

Brockman, Norbert. *An African Biographical Dictionary*. Santa Barbara, Calif.: ABC-CLIO, Inc., 1994.

Brook, Larry. *Cities through Time: Daily Life in Ancient and Modern Timbuktu*. Minneapolis: Runestone Press/Lerner Publishing, 1999.

Conlan, Roberta, managing editor. *Africa's Glorious Legacy* a volume of *Lost Civilizations*. Alexandria, Virginia: Time-Life Inc., 1994.

Chu, Daniel, and Elliot Skinner, Ph.D. *A Glorious Age In Africa: The Story Of Three Great African Empires.* Garden City, New York: Zenith Books/ Doubleday & Company, 1965.

Davidson, Basil. *Africa: History of a Continent.* New York: Macmillan, 1966.

_____. *Africa In History: Themes and Outlines.* New York: Macmillan, 1974 and 1991.

_____. *African Civilization Revisited: From Antiquity to Modern Times.* Trenton, New Jersey: Africa World Press, 1991.

_____. *The African Past: Chronicles from Antiquity to Modern Times.* Boston: Little, Brown and Company/Atlantic Monthly Press, 1964.

_____. *The Lost Cities of Africa.* Boston: Little, Brown and Company/ Atlantic Monthly Press, 1959.

_____. *The Search For Africa: History, Culture, Politics.* New York: Times Books/Random House, 1994.

_____. *The Story of Africa.* London: Mitchell Beazley, 1984.

Davidson, Basil, in collaboration with F.K. Buah, MA, and the advice of J.F. Ade Ajayi, BA, PhD. *The Growth Of African Civilization: A History of West Africa 1000 – 1800.* Essex, U.K.: Longman Group Limited, 1981.

Davidson, Basil, with F.K. Buah and the advice of J. F. Ade Ajayi. *A History Of West Africa: To The Nineteenth Century.* Garden City, New York: Anchor Books/Doubleday & Company, 1966.

Davidson, Basil, and the editors of Time-Life Books. *African Kingdoms.* Alexandria, Virginia: Time-Life Books, 1980.

DeGraft-Johnson, J.C. *African Glory: The Story of Vanished Negro Civilizations.* New York: Frederick A. Praeger, Inc., 1955.

de Gramont, Sanche. *The Strong Brown God: The Story Of The Niger River.* Boston: Houghton Mifflin, 1976.

de Villiers, Marq, and Sheila Hirtle. *Into Africa: A Journey Through the Ancient Empires.* Toronto: Key Porter Books, 1999.

Dietz, Betty Warner, and Michael Babatunde Olantunji. *Musical Instruments of Africa: Their Nature, Use, and Place in the Life of a Deeply Musical People.* New York: The John Day Company, 1965.

Dobler, Lavina, and William A. Brown, special consultant: Philip Curtin, Ph.D. *Great Rulers Of The African Past.* Garden City, New York: Zenith Books/Doubleday & Company, Inc., 1965.

Dubois, W.E.B. *The World and Africa.* Millwood, New York: Kraus-Thomson, 1976.

Durant, Will. *The Age Of Faith: A History of Medieval Civilization – Christian, Islamic, and Judaic – from Constantine to Dante: A.D. 325-1300.* New York: Simon and Schuster, 1950.

Durou, Jean-Marc, [editor]. *Sahara: The Forbidding Sands.* New York: Harry N. Abrams, Inc., 2000.

Eliade, Mircea, editor in chief. *The Encyclopedia of Religion*, vol. 10. New York: Macmillan, 1987.

Fage, J.D. *A History Of Africa*, a volume of *The History of Human Society.* London: Hutchinson & Co Ltd, 1978.

_____. *A History Of West Africa: An Introductory Survey*, 4th ed. Cambridge: Cambridge University Press, 1969.

Feeney, John. "Fortress of the Mountain". *Saudi Aramco World*. March-April, 1993: 32-9. http://www.saudiaramcoworld.com/issue/199302/fortress.of.the.mountain.htm

Garlake, Peter. *The Kingdoms of Africa*, a volume in *The Making of the Past*. Oxford: Elsevier-Phaidon/Phaidon Press, Ltd., 1978.

Gates, Jr., Henry Louis, *Wonders Of The African World.* New York: Alfred A. Knopf, 1999.

Gauthier-Pilters, Hilde, and Anne Innis Dagg. *The Camel: Its Evolution, Ecology, Behavior, and Relationship to Man*. Chicago: University of Chicago, 1981.

Hamilton, Paul author of Part 3. *Africa and Asia: Mapping Two Continents.* London: Aldus Books/Jupiter Books, 1973.

Hargreaves, John D. *West Africa: The Former French States*. Eaglewood Cliffs, New Jersey: Prentice-Hall, 1967.

Harris, Joseph E. *Africans And Their History*. New York: Meridian/Penguin Group, 1998.

Hutchinson, Louise Daniel. *Out of Africa: From West African Kingdoms to Colonization*. Washington D. C.: Smithsonian Institution Press, 1979.

Jackson, John G. *Introduction To African Civilizations.* New York: University Books, 1971.

Josephy, Jr., Alvin M., editor. *The Horizon History Of Africa*. New York: American Heritage/McGraw-Hill, Inc., 1971.

124

July, Robert W. *A History of the African People*. New York: Charles
  Scribner's Sons, 1974.

Labouret, Henri. *Africa Before the White Man*. New York: Walker and
  Company, 1962.

Levtzion, Nehemia. *Ancient Ghana and Mali*. New York: Africana Publishing
  Co./Holmes and Meier, 1980.

Lhote, Henri. *The Search for the Tassili Frescoes*. New York: E. P. Dutton
  & Co., Inc., 1959.

Luce, Henry R., editor in chief. *The World's Great Religions*. New York:
  Time, Inc., 1957.

McBride, Bunny. "Desert worship: Cool sanctuary in the ancient, earthen
  mosques of Mali. In this drought-ridden country, there is not the usual
  ablution fountain at each mosque's entryway. Here, visitors wash with
  sand," *The Christian Science Monitor*, 30 December 1988.

_____. "Salt of the Earth and Stars" *The Christian Science Monitor*, 26
  January 1983.

Mc Kissack, Patricia, and Fredrick. *The Royal Kingdoms of Ghana, Mali,
  and Songhay: Life in Medieval Africa*. New York: Henry Holt and
  Company, 1994.

Meltzer, Milton. *Ten Kings and the Worlds They Ruled*. New York: Orchard/
  Scholastic Inc., 2002.

Niani, D.T., editor. *General History of Africa·IV: Africa from the Twelfth to
  the Sixteenth Century*. Berkeley: University of California Press, 1984.

Niven, Sir Rex. *Nine Great Africans*. New York: Roy Publishers, 1964.

Oliver, Roland. *The African Experience*. London: George Weidenfeld and Nicolson, Ltd., 1991.

_____, editor. *The Cambridge History of Africa: Volume 3: from c. 1050 to c. 1600*. Cambridge: Cambridge University Press, 1977.

Oliver, Roland, and Michael Crowder, editors. *The Cambridge Encyclopedia of Africa*. Cambridge: Cambridge University Press, 1981.

Oliver, Roland, and Brian M. Fagan. *Africa in the Iron Age: c. 500 B.C. to 1400*. Cambridge: Cambridge University Press, 1975.

Oliver, Roland, and J. D. Fage. *A Short History of Africa*. New York: New York University Press, 1964.

Osae, T.A., S.N. Nwabara and A.T.O. Odunsi. *A Short History of West Africa: AD 1000 to the Present*. New York: Hill & Wang, 1973.

Pearson, R.A., E. Nengomasha and R. Krecek. "The challenges in using donkeys for work in Africa", *Meeting the challenges of animal traction*. London: Intermediate Technology Publications, 1999.

Pellow, Thomas. *The History of the Long Captivity and Adventures of Thomas Pellow, in South-Barbary*. New York and London: Garland Publishing, Inc., 1973.

Polatnick, Florence T., and Alberta L. Saletan. *Shapers of Africa*. New York: Julian Messner, 1972.

Raymond, André. *Cairo*. Cambridge, Massachusetts: Harvard University Press, 2000.

Reader, John. *Africa*. Washington D. C.: National Geographic, 2001.

_____, *Africa: A Biography Of The Continent*. New York: Alfred A. Knopf, 1998.

_____, *Africa: A companion to the P B S Series*. Washington D. C.: National Geographic, 2001.

Rodenbeck, John, editor. *Insight Guides: Cairo*. Maspeth, New York: Langenscheidt Publishers, Inc., 2002.

Romero, Orlando, and David Larkin. *Adobe: Building and Living With Adobe*. Boston · New York: Houghton Mifflin Company, 1994.

Samkange, Stanlake. *African Saga: a brief introduction to african history*. Nashville, Tennessee: Abingdon Press, 1971.

Shinnie, Margaret. *Ancient African Kingdoms*. New York: St. Martin's Press, 1965.

Stewart, Desmond. *Cairo: 5500 Years*. New York: Thomas Y. Crowell, 1968.

Thompson, Carol. *African Civilizations: The Empire of Mali*. New York: Franklin Watts, Grolier Publishing, 1998.

Van Sertima, Ivan. *The African presence in Ancient America: They Came Before Columbus*. New York: Random House, 1976.

Wilford, John Noble. "Project Digitizes Works From the Golden Age of Timbuktu," *The New York Times*, 20 May 2008.

Filmography

PBS Home Video, *Islam: Empire of Faith*, produced by Gardner Films in association with PBS and Devillier Donegan Enterprises. Robert Gardner, producer/director; series writer Jonathan Grupper. 2000.

Made in the USA
Monee, IL
30 August 2020